Ikenaga 2 Jos Leys

"A relatively simple formula can generate immensely complex images." – Jos Leys

Investigations

IN NUMBER, DATA, AND SPACE®

Polished Spiral Karin Kuhlmann

"Although the creation of fractals is bounded to strict mathematical rules, the results are always very inspiring." – **Karin Kuhlmann**

Investigations

IN NUMBER, DATA, AND SPACE®

Factors, Multiples, and Arrays

Investigation 3

Factors, Multiples, and Arrays

How Many in This Array?

How many cans are in this case, including those under the cap? __40__

How did you figure this out?

$8 \times 5 = 40$

Things That Come in Arrays

Think of things that come in arrays. For each thing you think of, fill in all four columns of the chart.

What Is It?	How Many in the Array?	Dimensions	Drawing of the Array

Addition Starter Problems

Solve each problem in two different
ways, using the first steps given.
Show your work clearly.

> **NOTE** Students practice strategies
> for addition. They work on efficiency
> and flexibility by solving the same
> problem in two different ways.
>
> **SMH** 8–9

---

1. 254 + 763 = ___1017___

   a. Start by solving 200 + 700.

```
 200    5^4    900
+700   ×6 3'  +117
 900    117   1017
```

b. Start by solving 250 + 750.

---

2. 627 + 575 = _____

   a. Start by solving 600 + 575.

b. Start by solving 27 + 75.

Ongoing Review

3. Find the missing number: 160, 260, 360, 460, _____

   A. 860   **B.** 560   **C.** 500   **D.** 480

Looking at Our Arrays

As you walk around and look at our class arrays, answer the following questions:

1. Which numbers have only one array?

2. Which numbers have a square array?

3. Which numbers have the most arrays?

Another Array Picture

How many cups of yogurt were in this case when it was full?

Yogurt Cups

4-Packs

_____ cups of yogurt

How did you figure this out?

Class Collections

Solve these problems. Be sure to write the equations that show how you got your answers.

NOTE Students practice addition in a story problem context.

SMH 8–9

1. **a.** The students in Ms. Chin's class are collecting bottle caps. They set a goal of collecting 400 bottle caps. This chart shows how many bottle caps they collected each week.

Week 1	Week 2	Week 3	Week 4
18	57	62	35

How many bottle caps did they collect by the end of 4 weeks?

   b. How many more bottle caps do they need to collect to reach 400?

2. **a.** Mr. Ruiz's class wants to collect 500 rocks for a science project. Students have brought in these numbers of rocks: 65, 38 and 29. How many rocks have they collected so far?

   b. How many more rocks do they need to collect to reach 500?

© Pearson Education 4

Coll____ting 1,000 Pennies

Solve t___e problems. Be sure to write the equations
that sh___ how you got your answers.

NOTE Students practice
addition in a story problem
context.

SMH 8–9

The st___ents in Ms. Shapiro's class want to collect
1,00___ennies in one month.

1. A___ the first week, they had collected 267 pennies.
H___ many more do they need to collect to reach 1,000?

2 ___fter two weeks, they had collected a total of 516 pennies.
How many more do they now need to reach 1,000?

After 3 weeks, they had collected a total of 843 pennies.
How many more do they need to collect in the last week
to reach 1,000?

Related Problem Sets

Solve the related problems in each set. As you work on these problems, think about how solving the first problem in each set may help you solve the others.

> **NOTE** Students solve addition and subtraction problems in related sets.
>
> **SMH** 13–15

1.

500	500	500
$-\ 85$	-185	-187

2. $400 - 200 = $ _____

$400 - 180 = $ _____

$420 - 180 = $ _____

---

3. $300 - 150 = $ _____

$350 - 150 = $ _____

$353 - 150 = $ _____

$353 - 147 = $ _____

4. $189 - 55 = $ _____

$189 - 155 = $ _____

$289 - 155 = $ _____

$289 - 165 = $ _____

---

5. $600 + $ _____ $= 1,000$

$650 + $ _____ $= 1,000$

$655 + $ _____ $= 1,000$

$658 + $ _____ $= 1,000$

6.

300	305	299
300	299	296
$+300$	$+296$	$+290$

Ongoing Review

7. Which does **not** equal 404?

A. $199 + 205$ **B.** $201 + 203$ **C.** $198 + 202$ **D.** $202 + 202$

What's on the Other Side? (page 1 of 2)

For each of the two Array Cards shown, figure out the number of squares in the array. Explain how you solved each problem.

How did you solve 8×8?

What's on the Other Side? (page 2 of 2)

How did you solve 7×9?

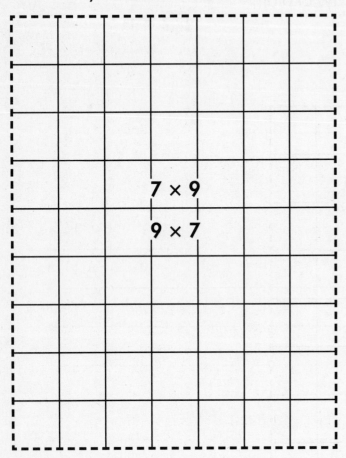

7×9

9×7

Multiple Turn Over Recording Sheet

Write the numbers of your 10 Multiple Cards on the blank
cards. As each factor is called, record it in the factor list.
Then write which multiples of that number you have among
your cards.

Game 1 Multiple Cards

□ □ □ □ □ □ □ □ □ □

Factor	Multiple Cards I Can Turn Over
1. _____	_____
2. _____	_____
3. _____	_____
4. _____	_____
5. _____	_____

Game 2 Multiple Cards

□ □ □ □ □ □ □ □ □ □

Factor	Multiple Cards I Can Turn Over
1. _____	_____
2. _____	_____
3. _____	_____
4. _____	_____
5. _____	_____

Distance Problems

NOTE Students practice addition in a story problem context, finding a combination of addends that equals a given sum.

 SMH 8–9

1. **a.** Elena's family is taking a bicycle vacation over 4 days. They plan to bicycle 115 miles in all. Write an addition equation that shows one possible combination of miles they could bike over 4 days.

   _____ + _____ + _____ + _____ = 115

   b. Write another equation to show a second way they could bike a total of 115 miles.

   _____ + _____ + _____ + _____ = 115

2. **a.** Edwin and his family are driving to a family reunion 516 miles away. They have 3 days to drive the total distance. Write an addition equation that shows one possible combination of miles they could drive over 3 days.

   _____ + _____ + _____ = 516

   b. Write another equation to show a second way they could drive a total of 516 miles.

   _____ + _____ + _____ = 516

Ongoing Review

3. 124 + 127 + 125 = _____

   A. 376   **B.** 375   **C.** 372   **D.** 366

Practicing with Multiplication Cards (page 1 of 2)

NOTE Students are learning the multiplication combinations (or "facts") up to 12 × 12. Help your child practice these.

SMH 29–34

1. Look at the front of each Multiplication Card. If you have a helper, that person can show you one card at a time.

2. Your job is to say the answer to the problem as quickly as you can. If you get the answer right away, put the card in a pile of combinations that you "just know." If you have to stop and figure it out, put it into a different pile of combinations that you are still "working on."

3. Paper-clip your "just know" cards together, and set them aside.

4. Look at each card in your "working on" pile. Think of an easy multiplication combination, one that you already know, that can help you remember each one. Write it on the line that says "Start with _____."

   Example: "For 6 × 7, I know that 7 × 7 = 49, so it must be one 7 less—that's 42."

   6×7
   7×6
   Start with ___7 × 7___

5. Go through each of the cards in your "working on" pile at least 3 times, using your "start with" combinations to help you find the answers.

6. Put all of your cards back together, both "just know" and "working on," and go through them again.

7. Over the next few weeks, keep practicing until you have no more cards in your "working on" pile. Practice at school when you have extra time, and practice at home with a family member.

Practicing with Multiplication Cards (page 2 of 2)

1. Which multiplication combinations are you practicing?

_____   _____

_____   _____

_____   _____

_____   _____

2. Write two multiplication combinations that are hard for you, and explain what helps you remember them.

Multiplication combination: _____

What helps me:

_____

_____

_____

Multiplication combination: _____

What helps me:

_____

_____

_____

3. How did you practice your multiplication combinations? Who helped you?

_____

_____

_____

Money Problems

Solve these problems. Show clearly how you solved each one.

> **NOTE** Students practice addition and subtraction in the context of money.
>
> **SMH** 11–12

1. $6.57 + $4.98 = _____

2. $7.34 + $2.78 = _____

3. $8.60 − $3.95 = _____

4. $7.30 − $4.75 = _____

Ongoing Review

5. One pen costs $1.55. What is the total cost of 3 pens?

   A. $3.65   **B.** $4.55   **C.** $4.65   **D.** $5.55

More Practice with Multiplication Cards

NOTE Students are learning the multiplication combinations (multiplication "facts") to 12×12. Continue helping your child with this practice.

SMH 29–34

1. Which multiplication combinations are you practicing?

_____   _____

_____   _____

_____   _____

2. Write two multiplication combinations that are hard for you, and explain what helps you remember them.

Multiplication combination: _____

What helps me:

_____

_____

Multiplication combination: _____

What helps me:

_____

_____

3. How did you practice your multiplication combinations? Who helped you?

_____

_____

_____

NO   tudents solve
mult   addition and
subt   n problems in
a st   oblem context.

SM   9, 13–15

Story Problems

Solve these problems. Show how you got
your answers.

1. Marisa had 574 stamps in her stamp collection.
She gave 255 stamps to her brother to start his
own collection. Then Marisa's aunt gave her
449 stamps. How many stamps does Marisa
have in her collection now?

2. Ms. Gomez is running for the city council. She printed
1,000 campaign brochures for the elections. On the first
day, she gave away 387 brochures. On the second day,
she gave away 515 brochures. How many brochures
does she have left?

3. a. Devon earned $13.50 for babysitting his niece. He
also earned $4.50 for doing his chores that week.
He wants to buy a backpack that costs $18.45.
Does he have enough money?

   b. If he does not have enough money, how much more
   does he need?

Factors, Multiples, and Arrays   Homework

Factors of Multiples of 100 (page 1 of 2)

Fill in each chart on these two pages. Tell how many of the given factor it takes to get to each multiple of 100. Then write the factor pair. Look at the first two charts for examples. Use multiplication combinations you know, or use math tools, such as the 300 chart, to help you.

> **NOTE** Students are working on finding factors of 100, 200, 300, and other multiples of 100. Here, they find ways to multiply to make these numbers.
>
> **SMH** 29-34

Factor	How Many?	Multiple	Factor Pair	Factor	How Many?	Multiple	Factor Pair
2	50	100	2 × 50	5	20	100	5 × 20
2		200		5		200	
2		300		5		300	
2		400		5		400	
2		500		5		500	
2		600		5		600	

Polished Spiral Karin Kuhlmann

"Although the creation of fractals is bounded to strict mathematical rules, the results are always very inspiring." – **Karin Kuhlmann**

Investigations
IN NUMBER, DATA, AND SPACE®

Describing the Shape of the Data

Multiplication Combinations of 3s, 6s, and 12s

NOTE: Students practice multiplication combinations ("facts"). They look for patterns in the 3s, 6s, and 12s combinations.

SMH 29–34

1. Solve these problems.

$1 \times 3 =$

$2 \times 3 =$ $1 \times 6 =$

$3 \times 3 =$

$4 \times 3 =$ $2 \times 6 =$ $1 \times 12 =$

$5 \times 3 =$

$6 \times 3 =$ $3 \times 6 =$

$7 \times 3 =$

$8 \times 3 =$ $4 \times 6 =$ $2 \times 12 =$

$9 \times 3 =$

$10 \times 3 =$ $5 \times 6 =$

$11 \times 3 =$

$12 \times 3 =$ $6 \times 6 =$ $3 \times 12 =$

2. What patterns do you notice?

3. Ask someone at home to help you practice the multiplication combinations that you are working on.

Party Supplies

Solve each of the story problems below.
Show your thinking.

NOTE Students practice solving multiplication problems in a story context.

1. Ms. Ruiz bought 13 packages of cups for a big party. Each package contains 8 cups. How many cups did she buy?

2. Ms. Ruiz bought 9 packages of plates for the party. Each package contains 12 plates. How many plates did she buy?

3. Ms. Ruiz bought 7 packages of napkins for the party. Each package contains 16 napkins. How many napkins did she buy?

Ongoing Review

4. Which product is greater than 70?

   A. 7×9 **C.** 5×11

   B. 6×12 **D.** 8×8

Describing the Shape of the Data

Related Multiplication Combinations

Solve each set of related problems below.

NOTE Students solve sets of related multiplication combinations. Encourage them to solve each problem mentally.

 SMH 29–34

1.

$5 \times 7 =$ _____

$10 \times 7 =$ _____

2.

$9 \times 10 =$ _____

$9 \times 12 =$ _____

3.

$7 \times 6 =$ _____

$7 \times 7 =$ _____

4.

$4 \times 8 =$ _____

$8 \times 8 =$ _____

$12 \times 8 =$ _____

5.

$4 \times 6 =$ _____

$8 \times 6 =$ _____

$12 \times 6 =$ _____

6.

$6 \times 8 =$ _____

$7 \times 8 =$ _____

$8 \times 8 =$ _____

7.

$10 \times 10 =$ _____

$11 \times 11 =$ _____

$12 \times 12 =$ _____

8.

$12 \times 3 =$ _____

$12 \times 6 =$ _____

$12 \times 9 =$ _____

9.

$6 \times 6 =$ _____

$8 \times 6 =$ _____

$10 \times 6 =$ _____

10.

$11 \times 4 =$ _____

$11 \times 6 =$ _____

$11 \times 10 =$ _____

11.

$7 \times 5 =$ _____

$7 \times 6 =$ _____

$7 \times 11 =$ _____

12.

$9 \times 5 =$ _____

$9 \times 7 =$ _____

$9 \times 9 =$ _____

Factors

For each of the following numbers, list as many pairs of factors as you can.

NOTE Students practice multiplication combinations ("facts") by finding pairs of factors for a given product.

SMH 22, 23

Example: 28	24
_2_ × _14_	____ × ____
_4_ × _7_	____ × ____
____ × ____	____ × ____

32	18
____ × ____	____ × ____
____ × ____	____ × ____
____ × ____	____ × ____

16	20
____ × ____	____ × ____
____ × ____	____ × ____
____ × ____	____ × ____

Describing the Shape of the Data   Homework

How Many Cavities?

How many cavities have you had?

NOTE Students are gathering data about the number of cavities they have had for a class data collection.

SMH 87

© Pearson Education 4

Comparing the Heights of First and Fourth Graders

1. How do the heights of the first-graders compare with the heights of the fourth graders in your class? Write three statements about this question.

In your statements include ideas about the data such as these: Where are there lots of data? How big are clumps of data? What are the tallest heights and the shortest heights? What outliers are there? What do you think are the typical heights of first graders and of fourth graders?

a. _____

b. _____

c. _____

2. About how much taller do you think a fourth grader is than a first grader? Why do you think so? Support your ideas with evidence from the data.

_____

_____

_____

_____

_____

Counting Around the Class

NOTE Students find the multiples of a given number and solve multiplication problems.

SMH 25

1. Mr. Patel's students counted by 5s. The first person said 5, the second said 10, and the third said 15. Each student said one number.

How many students counted to get to 100? _____

How do you know?

2. Ms. Bailey's students counted by 10s. The first person said 10, the second said 20, and the third said 30. Each student said one number.

a. How many students counted to get to 270? _____

How do you know?

b. When Ms. Bailey's students counted by 10s, did anyone say the number 225? _____

How do you know?

Ongoing Review

3. Which has the same product as 3×12?

A. 8×4 **C.** 6×6

B. 6×24 **D.** 9×6

Things That Come in Groups

> **NOTE** Students practice multiplication by solving story problems.
>
> **SMH** 16, 17

Solve the story problems below. Write a multiplication equation for each problem and show how you solved it.

Spiders have 8 legs.

1. How many legs are on 5 spiders? _____

Equation: _____ $5 \times 8 =$ _____

2. How many legs are on 11 spiders? _____

Equation: _____

3. How many legs are on 16 spiders? _____

Equation: _____

Ongoing Review

4. Which is **not** a factor of 54?

  A. 3   **C.** 8

  B. 6   **D.** 9

Developing a Survey Question (page 1 of 3)

1. Choose a survey question.

   Think about a question that will:
   - Help you compare two groups of people.
   - Result in numerical data.
   - Give you data that you are interested in.
   - Help you find out something that you don't know.

   Decide on a question for your survey. Write your question.

   _____

   _____

2. Try out and revise your question.

   Ask three students your survey question. Talk with them and your partner about making changes to your question.

   Think about the following:
   - Did the students understand your question?
   - Were they able to respond to your question without further explanation from you?
   - Did their responses give you the information you were interested in?

   If you revise your question, write it here.

   _____

   _____

Developing a Survey Question (page 2 of 3)

3. Plan your survey and make predictions.

   a. You will compare the responses to your question from two groups of students. Which two groups of students will you compare?

   _____

   _____

   _____

   b. What do you want to find out from comparing these two groups of students?

   _____

   _____

   _____

   _____

   c. What do you predict you will find when you compare the responses of these two groups of students? Why do you think this will be the result?

   _____

   _____

   _____

Developing a Survey Question (page 3 of 3)

4. Plan how to collect and record your data.

Think about the following:

- How are you going to record the data as you collect them?
- What information do you need to write?
- How are you going to keep track of which people you have asked?
- Who is going to do what?

Write how you will record and keep track of your data.

_____

_____

_____

_____

_____

_____

_____

Peanut Count

Each of the students in Mr. Herrera's class took a handful of trail mix and counted the number of peanuts.

> **NOTE** Students represent data in a line plot.
>
> **SMH** 88–89

1. Make a line plot of the data.

Peanut Count			
Benson	8	Yuson	6
Yuki	5	Anna	7
Noemi	6	Helena	9
Derek	13	LaTanya	8
Bill	10	Marisol	9
Abdul	9	Andrew	8
Steve	8	Ursula	10
Damian	8	Sabrina	6
Lucy	8	Richard	6

2. If you took a handful of the same trail mix, how many peanuts do you think you would get? Explain why you think so.

_____

_____

Ongoing Review

3. What is the highest number of peanuts a student counted?

A. 13   **B.** 7   **C.** 6   **D.** 5

14

How Many Cubes Can Students Grab? (page 1 of 2)

Students in a third-grade class collected data about how many cubes kindergarteners and third graders could grab with one hand. They put their data in two bar graphs.

NOTE In this homework, students look carefully at the shapes of two different sets of data and compare them.

SMH 94–97

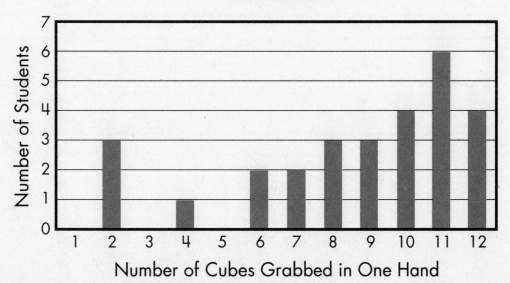

How Many Cubes Can Students Grab? (page 2 of 2)

1. Write three statements about the number of cubes third graders and kindergartners grabbed.

a. _____

_____

b. _____

_____

c. _____

_____

2. How many cubes would you say a kindergartner typically grabs? Why would you say this is typical?

_____

_____

3. How many cubes would you say a third grader typically grabs? Why would you say this is typical?

_____

_____

© Pearson Education 4

Interesting Plot

Ollie counted the number of houses on each block between home and school. The line plot shows Ollie's data.

NOTE Students describe features of a set of data on a line plot.

SMH 88, 89, 90, 91

1. What seems to be the typical number of houses? Explain why you think so.

_____

_____

_____

_____

2. An *outlier* is a piece of data that "lies outside" the rest of the data. Are there any outliers? If so, what is it and what might account for this unusual piece of data?

_____

_____

_____

Ongoing Review

3. How many blocks have 11 houses?

   A. 1   **B.** 2   **C.** 3   **D.** 4

Missing Factors

Fill in the missing factors in these problems.

NOTE Students practice multiplication combinations ("facts") in related sets.

SMH **29–34**

1.	**2.**	**3.**
$6 \times \underline{\hspace{2cm}} = 36$	$9 \times \underline{\hspace{2cm}} = 36$	$\underline{\hspace{2cm}} \times 12 = 36$
$6 \times \underline{\hspace{2cm}} = 72$	$9 \times \underline{\hspace{2cm}} = 72$	$\underline{\hspace{2cm}} \times 12 = 72$

4.	**5.**	**6.**
$\underline{\hspace{2cm}} \times 8 = 48$	$11 \times \underline{\hspace{2cm}} = 44$	$6 \times \underline{\hspace{2cm}} = 48$
$\underline{\hspace{2cm}} \times 8 = 88$	$11 \times \underline{\hspace{2cm}} = 88$	$6 \times \underline{\hspace{2cm}} = 54$

7.	**8.**	**9.**
$9 \times \underline{\hspace{2cm}} = 45$	$\underline{\hspace{2cm}} \times 7 = 21$	$\underline{\hspace{2cm}} \times 8 = 40$
$9 \times \underline{\hspace{2cm}} = 54$	$\underline{\hspace{2cm}} \times 7 = 42$	$\underline{\hspace{2cm}} \times 8 = 48$
$9 \times \underline{\hspace{2cm}} = 63$	$\underline{\hspace{2cm}} \times 7 = 84$	$\underline{\hspace{2cm}} \times 8 = 56$

10.	**11.**	**12.**
$7 \times \underline{\hspace{2cm}} = 28$	$6 \times \underline{\hspace{2cm}} = 36$	$\underline{\hspace{2cm}} \times 12 = 48$
$7 \times \underline{\hspace{2cm}} = 35$	$8 \times \underline{\hspace{2cm}} = 64$	$\underline{\hspace{2cm}} \times 12 = 60$
$7 \times \underline{\hspace{2cm}} = 63$	$12 \times \underline{\hspace{2cm}} = 144$	$\underline{\hspace{2cm}} \times 12 = 108$

Related Multiplication Combinations

Solve the following problems.

NOTE Students practice multiplication combinations ("facts") in related sets.

 29–34

1.

$5 \times 8 =$ _____

$10 \times 8 =$ _____

2.

$11 \times 10 =$ _____

$11 \times 12 =$ _____

3.

$7 \times 4 =$ _____

$7 \times 8 =$ _____

4.

$4 \times 6 =$ _____

$8 \times 6 =$ _____

$12 \times 6 =$ _____

5.

$4 \times 9 =$ _____

$8 \times 9 =$ _____

$12 \times 9 =$ _____

6.

$6 \times 6 =$ _____

$7 \times 7 =$ _____

$8 \times 8 =$ _____

7.

$10 \times 12 =$ _____

$11 \times 12 =$ _____

$12 \times 12 =$ _____

8.

$8 \times 3 =$ _____

$8 \times 6 =$ _____

$8 \times 9 =$ _____

9.

$6 \times 6 =$ _____

$8 \times 6 =$ _____

$10 \times 6 =$ _____

10.

$11 \times 5 =$ _____

$11 \times 6 =$ _____

$11 \times 11 =$ _____

11.

$7 \times 5 =$ _____

$7 \times 6 =$ _____

$7 \times 12 =$ _____

12.

$12 \times 5 =$ _____

$12 \times 7 =$ _____

$12 \times 9 =$ _____

What Did You Learn From Your Survey? (page 1 of 2)

1. What was your survey question?

   _____

   _____

2. Suppose that a teacher was interested in your survey
   and asked, "What did you learn from your survey?"
   Write at least three things you learned. Give evidence
   from the data.

   _____

   _____

   _____

   _____

   _____

   _____

   _____

What Did You Learn From Your Survey? (page 2 of 2)

3. How did the results of your survey compare with your predictions?

_____

_____

_____

_____

4. Now that you have learned some things about your question, can you think of some other survey questions that you would ask to learn more about this topic?

_____

_____

_____

_____

5. What else did you learn about data investigations from doing this project?

_____

_____

_____

_____

Division With Remainders

NOTE Students practice solving division problems and interpreting remainders in story problem contexts.

SMH 47, 48–49

1. Fifty people are waiting in line for the roller coaster. Each car holds 8 people. How many cars will the 50 people fill?

   Division equation: _____ ÷ _____ = _____   Answer: _____

2. Forty people bought tickets for a boat ride. Twelve people can ride in a boat at a time. How many boats will the 40 people fill?

   Division equation: _____ ÷ _____ = _____   Answer: _____

3. How many prizes could you get with 50 tickets?

   Division equation:

   _____ ÷ _____ = _____

   Answer: _____

ARCADE PRIZES

6 Tickets per prize!

4. The students in Mr. Brown's class counted around the class by 5s. Each student said one number. The number they ended with was 65. How many students counted?

   Division equation: _____ ÷ _____ = _____   Answer: _____

Ongoing Review

5. The students in Ms. Jones' class counted around the class by 4s. Each student said one number. There are 29 students in her class. Which of these numbers did they say?

   A. 120   **B.** 100   **C.** 50   **D.** 10

Arranging Cans of Juice (page 1 of 2)

NOTE Students find factors by arranging numbers into rectangular arrays.

 SMH 18, 23

Solve the following problems.

1. **a.** You have 28 cans of juice. Show all of the ways you can arrange these cans into arrays. Draw the arrays in the space below.

   b. List all of the factors of 28.

Arranging Cans
of Juice (page 2 of 2)

2. **a.** Mauricio has 42 cans of juice. Show all of the
ways he can arrange his cans into arrays. Draw the
arrays in the space below.

b. List all of the factors of 42.

Mystery Data A

The table and graph below show the same data.
These data represent some group of living things.

Individual	Inches	Individual	Inches	Individual	Inches
A	84	I	84	Q	81
B	83	J	84	R	79
C	78	K	85	S	75
D	75	L	82	T	76
E	90	M	78	U	83
F	77	N	83	V	81
G	75	O	72	W	78
H	81	P	80	X	78

Heights or Lengths of Members of a Group of Living Things in Inches

1. What is the median height or length of this group?
   Are the data clustered around the median or spread out?

   _____

   _____

2. What do you think the group could be? Give reasons
   for your answer.

   _____

   _____

   _____

Mystery Data B

The table and graph below show the same data.
These data represent some group of living things.

Individual	Inches	Individual	Inches	Individual	Inches
A	78	G	86	M	84
B	96	H	93	N	80
C	114	I	64	O	72
D	94	J	54	P	54
E	63	K	72	Q	79
F	72	L	108	R	116

Heights or Lengths of Members of a Group of Living Things in Inches

1. What is the median height or length of this group?
Are the data clustered around the median or spread out?

_____

_____

2. What do you think the group could be? Give reasons
for your answer.

_____

_____

_____

_____

Mystery Data C ✏️

This information is about a group of living things:

- The median height or length of these living things is 19.5 inches.

- The shortest height or length in this group is 18 inches.

- The tallest height or length in this group is 22 inches.

- There are 30 individuals in this group.

1. Make a line plot of the heights or lengths of these living things. Decide where you think the 30 pieces of data might belong, according to the information above.

2. What do you think the group could be? Give reasons for your answer.

_____

_____

_____

_____

_____

NOTE Students represent and describe a set of data.

SMH **88–91**

Parking Lot Data

The students in Ms. May's class counted the cars in the school parking lot at the beginning of every school day for a month.

1. Represent the data in a table, a line plot, or with tallies.

Number of Cars in the Parking Lot				
18	23	22	25	20
23	19	17	24	23
22	23	25	24	24
22	23	22	24	25

2. Describe the data. Try to include a discussion of the range, how it clumps or spreads out, whether there are any outliers, and what is typical.

_____

_____

_____

_____

Ongoing Review

3. What is the median number of cars in the parking lot?

A. 20   **B.** 21   **C.** 22   **D.** 23

Things That Come in Groups

Solve the story problems below. Write a
multiplication equation for each problem,
and show how you solved it.

NOTE Students solve
multiplication problems
and write an equation to
represent each problem.

SMH 16, 17

Insects have 6 legs.

1. How many legs do 9 insects have? _____

   Equation: _____

2. How many legs do 11 insects have? _____

   Equation: _____

3. How many legs do 20 insects have? _____

   Equation: _____

Comparing WNBA Players' Points Per Game (page 1 of 2)

Yolanda Griffith and Mwadi Mabika both played basketball in the WNBA (Women's National Basketball Association). They each scored points during most of the games they played in the 2003 season.

Here is a line plot of the points Mabika scored in each of the 40 games she played in the 2003 season:

0 1 2 3 4 5 6 7 8 9 10 11 12 13 14 15 16 17 18 19 20 21 22 23 24 25 26 27 28

Points Mabika Scored per Game

Below are the points Griffith scored during each of the 39 games she played in the 2003 season. Make a line plot of her points per game:

10 15 12 17 20 27 17 12 10 8 19 19 6 7 12 16 21
22 22 11 24 20 15 17 18 7 27 15 22 13 6 4 15 11 7

Points Griffith Scored per Game

© Pearson Education 4

Comparing WNBA Players' Points Per Game (page 2 of 2)

1. What is the median of Mabika's points per game? _____
   How did you figure out the median?

   _____

   _____

   _____

2. What is the median of Griffith's points per game? _____
   How did you figure out the median?

   _____

   _____

   _____

3. How do the number of points Griffith scored in the
   games she played in the 2003 season compare with
   the number of points Mabika scored? Write at least
   three statements that compare Mabika's points-per-
   game with Griffith's points-per-game.

   Consider where the data are concentrated, the highest
   and lowest numbers of points scored, the outliers, and
   the medians.

   1. _____

      _____

   2. _____

      _____

   3. _____

      _____

How Heavy is Your Pumpkin?

NOTE Students practice representing and describing data.

SMH 88–93

Damian grew eighteen pumpkins and recorded their weights when he picked them.

1. Organize the data in a line plot or other graph.

Pumpkin Weights in Pounds

7   10   4   6   9   3   11   4

12

12   4   2   11   4

3

3   11   2

2. Describe how the data is spread out by finding the median and other measures, such as the range. Discuss whether you think the median *alone* provides a good description of the data and why.

_____

_____

_____

_____

Ongoing Review

3. Half of the pumpkins weigh less than

A. 5 pounds   **B.** 4 pounds   **C.** 3 pounds   **D.** 2 pounds

Is This a Good Game? (page 1 of 2)

Use Mabika's and Griffith's points per game to answer the
following questions.

1. Barney, who is a big fan of Mwadi Mabika, went
   to her game on May 28. Mabika scored 10 points.
   Barney wants to know whether this was a good game
   or a bad game for Mabika. What is your opinion?
   Use the data to support your opinion.

   _____

   _____

   _____

2. Venetta, who is a big fan of Yolanda Griffith, went to
   her game on July 5. Griffith scored 17 points. Venetta
   wants to know whether this was a good game or a
   bad game for Griffith. What is your opinion? Use the
   data to support your opinion.

   _____

   _____

   _____

3. Suppose that you were an owner of a team who was
   thinking about hiring Mwadi Mabika or Yolanda Griffith.
   As you decide whom to hire, one of the things you want
   to look at carefully is the player's points per game.
   According to their point scoring data, which player do
   you think you might hire for your basketball team? Why?

   _____

   _____

Is This a Good Game? (page 2 of 2)

4. Suppose that a sports reporter is writing a story comparing the points Yolanda Griffith and Mwadi Mabika scored during the 2003 season. The reporter is planning to report their median scores. What can the reporter's readers learn from a comparison of their median scores?

_____

_____

_____

_____

_____

_____

_____

5. Do you think this is enough information for readers to know about Griffith's and Mabika's scoring records? If not, what other information do you think the reporter should include?

_____

_____

_____

_____

_____

_____

Multiplication Pairs

NOTE Students practice solving multiplication problems.

SMH 16–17

1. Solve each pair of multiplication problems below.

   Use the first problem to help you solve the second problem.

12 × 8 = _____	15 × 6 = _____
24 × 8 = _____	30 × 3 = _____
15 × 4 = _____	9 × 9 = _____
15 × 8 = _____	18 × 9 = _____
32 × 5 = _____	8 × 6 = _____
16 × 10 = _____	16 × 6 = _____

Ongoing Review

2. Which of the following does not equal 12 × 8?

   A. 24 × 4   **C.** 3 × 28

   B. 2 × 48   **D.** 6 × 16

Describing the Shape of the Data   Homework

Height Comparisons
(page 1 of 2)

A few days ago, you looked at some heights and lengths of different animals and people. Look at the following heights and lengths:

> **NOTE** Students use a set of data to answer questions about the lengths or heights of members of a group of living things.
>
> **SMH** 11–12

Names	Heights/Lengths
Vince Carter (basketball player)	78 inches
Shaquille O'Neal (basketball player)	85 inches
Baby 1	18 inches
Baby 2	22 inches
Fourth grader	64 inches
Shannon (boa constrictor)	116 inches
Black cottonwood (tree)	1,764 inches

1. Who is the taller basketball player? _____

   Who is the shorter baby? _____

   How much taller is the taller basketball player than the

   shorter baby? _____ Show your work.

Height Comparisons
(page 2 of 2)

2. Look at the fourth grader and Shannon. How much longer is Shannon than the fourth grader is tall? _____ Show your work.

3. How tall are you? _____ Find someone or something that is at least 20" taller than you. What is it? _____ How much taller is it? _____ Show your work.

4. Look at the black cottonwood and the fourth grader. How much taller is the black cottonwood than the fourth grader? _____ Show your work.

How Many People Counted?

NOTE Students find the multiples of a given number and solve multiplication problems.

SMH 25

In these counting problems, each student said one number.

1. The students in Ms. Alonzo's class counted by 20s. The first student said 20, the second student said 40, and the third said 60. How many students counted to get to 300? _____ How do you know?

2. The students in Mr. Nelson's class counted by 15s. The first student said 15, the second student said 30, and the third said 45. How many students counted to get to 300? _____ How do you know?

3. The students in Ms. Weinberg's class counted by 25s. The first student said 25, the second student said 50, and the third student said 75.

   a. How many students counted to get to 300? _____ How do you know?

   b. When the students in Ms. Weinberg's class counted by 25s, did anyone say the number 180? _____ How do you know?

Creating a Likelihood Line (page 1 of 2)

> **NOTE** Students are beginning a study of probability. They are placing events according to their likelihood.
>
> **SMH** 98

Think about the neighborhood in which you live. Can you think of any events in the future that you are *certain* will happen? Write them on the likelihood line on the next page.

Add any events that would be *impossible*.

Now add a few events that are *unlikely* to occur, that *maybe* will occur, and that are *likely* to occur. You may want to ask family members or friends to help you think of events and where they might go on the line.

Now answer the questions below. Use examples from your Likelihood Line.

1. If something is unlikely to happen, does this mean that it will never happen? _____
What would you think if it did happen?

_____

_____

_____

2. If something is likely to happen, does this mean that it will always happen? _____
What would you think if it did not happen?

_____

_____

_____

_____

Creating a Likelihood Line (page 2 of 2)

Describing the Shape of the Data

Placing Events on the Likelihood Line (page 1 of 2)

Put the letter of each event on the Likelihood Line above.
Explain your reasoning.

1. **Event A** The probability of flipping a coin and getting heads.
   Explain why you put it where you did.

   _____

   _____

2. **Event B** The probability of rolling a number cube and getting a 6.
   Explain why you put it where you did.

   _____

   _____

3. **Event C** The probability of rolling a number cube once and getting either a 1, a 2, or a 3.
   Explain why you put it where you did.

   _____

   _____

Placing Events on the Likelihood Line (page 2 of 2)

4. **Event D** the probability of pulling a blue cube out of a bag that contains 1 red cube and 99 blue cubes.
   Explain why you put it where you did.

   _____

   _____

5. **Event E** the probability of pulling a girl's name out of a container that holds the names of all of the students in the class.
   Explain why you put it where you did.

   _____

   _____

6. **Event F** the probability of pulling a boy's name out of the same container.
   Explain why you put it where you did.

   _____

   _____

7. **Event G** the probability of pulling your name out of the same container.
   Explain why you put it where you did.

   _____

   _____

Comparing Test Scores

These line plots show two students' scores
for 12 science tests.

NOTE Students order and
find the median of data sets.

 92–93

Anna's Science Tests

Jill's Science Tests

1. Find the median score for each student.

Anna _____   Jill _____

2. Overall, which student do you think had better scores?

_____

Why do you think so?

_____

_____

_____

_____

Ongoing Review

3. On how many tests did Anna score more than 83?

A. 1   **B.** 3   **C.** 6   **D.** 7

Describing the Shape of the Data   Homework

Counting Around the Class

In these counting problems, each student said
one number.

NOTE Students use their
knowledge of multiples to
solve these related problems.

 25

1. The students in Ms. Alonzo's class counted by 5s.
The first student said 5, the second student said 10,
and the third said 15. How many students

counted to get to 250? _____
How do you know?

2. The students in Mr. Nelson's class counted by 10s.
The first student said 10, the second student said 20,
and the third said 30. How many students counted

to get to 250? _____
How do you know?

3. a. The students in Ms. Weinberg's class counted by
25s. The first student said 25, the second student
said 50, and the third student said 75. How many

students counted to get to 250? _____
How do you know?

b. When the students in Ms. Weinberg's class counted
by 25s, did anyone say 200? _____
How do you know?

© Pearson Education 4

Record of Cubes in a Bag

1. Record how many of each color cube are in your bag.

_____ red cubes   _____ blue cubes

2. Prediction: How many times do you think you will pull a red cube out of the bag?

3. Record which color you pull out on each trial.

4. Total number of red cubes: _____

Arranging Cans of Juice

NOTE Students find factors by arranging numbers into rectangular arrays.

 23

1. **a.** You have 32 cans of juice. Show all the ways you can arrange these cans into arrays. Draw the arrays in the space below.

2. **a.** Mauricio has 36 cans of juice. Show all the ways he can arrange his cans into arrays. Draw the arrays in the space below.

b. List all the factors of 32.

b. List all the factors of 36.

Ongoing Review

3. Which number is prime?

   A. 49   **B.** 27   **C.** 17   **D.** 9

Comparing Probability Experiments (page 1 of 2)

Experiment 1: 10 red cubes and 10 blue cubes

1. How many red cubes did you draw in 50 trials? _____

2. Did the number you got surprise you, or is it about what you expected? Why?

   _____

   _____

3. Look at the class line plot. What do you notice about the data for Experiment 1?

   _____

   _____

Experiment 2: 5 red cubes and 15 blue cubes

4. How many red cubes did you draw in 50 trials? _____

5. Did the number you got surprise you, or is it about what you expected? Why?

   _____

   _____

6. Look at the class line plot. What do you notice about the data for Experiment 2?

   _____

   _____

   _____

Describing the Shape of the Data

Comparing Probability Experiments (page 2 of 2)

Experiment 3: 15 red cubes and 5 blue cubes

7. How many red cubes did you draw in 50 trials? _____

8. Did the number you got surprise you, or is it about what you expected? Why?

_____

_____

9. Look at the class line plot. What do you notice about the data for Experiment 3?

_____

_____

10. What do you notice when you compare the results from the three experiments?

_____

_____

_____

_____

Leg Riddles

Birds have 2 legs.
Dogs have 4 legs.
Ladybugs have 6 legs.

NOTE Students solve multiplication and division problems in story problem contexts.

1. There are 48 legs, and they all belong to dogs.
   How many dogs are there?

2. There are 3 ladybugs, 7 dogs, and 13 birds in the
   house. How many legs are there altogether?

3. There are 36 legs in the house. All the legs belong
   to birds, dogs, and ladybugs. How many of each
   creature—birds, dogs, and ladybugs—might be in
   the house?

   (There are many possible answers. How many can
   you find?)

Birds	Dogs	Ladybugs

Don't Miss The Bus!

Josh takes the bus to school every day. The bus is
supposed to arrive at his stop at 7:30. For one month,
Josh notes the times that the bus arrives in the morning.
The table shows the data he collected.

NOTE Students solve
real-world problems
involving the math
content of this unit.

SMH 88–91

7:30	7:28	7:31	7:29	7:36
7:40	7:31	7:28	7:35	7:31
7:36	7:33	7:35	7:29	7:31
7:34	7:36	7:29	7:33	7:30

1. Make a line plot of the data Josh collected. Remember
to label your line plot.

2. What time will the bus most likely arrive? Why do you
think so?

3. What time does Josh need to be at the bus stop to
make sure he does not miss the bus? Use the data from
the line plot to explain your thinking.

Polished Spiral Karin Kuhlmann

"Although the creation of fractals is bounded to strict mathematical rules, the results are always very inspiring." – **Karin Kuhlmann**

Investigations
IN NUMBER, DATA, AND SPACE®

Multiple Towers and Division Stories

Practice with Multiplication Cards 2

NOTE Students are working on the multiplication combinations (facts) to 12 × 12. Help your child with this practice.

SMH 33–34

1. Which multiplication combinations are you practicing?

_____

_____

_____

2. Write two multiplication combinations that are hard for you, and explain what helps you remember them.

Multiplication combination: _____

What helps me: _____

_____

_____

Multiplication combination: _____

What helps me: _____

_____

_____

3. How did you practice your multiplication combinations? Who helped you?

_____

_____

_____

Multiple To   and Division Stories

About Our Multiple Tower (page 1 of 2)

Answer t   e questions about the multiple tower that you
and your   rtner built.

1. What   mber did you use to build your multiple tower? _____

2. What   he ending multiple on your tower? _____

3. How   y multiples are in your tower? _____

4. What   ne way to figure out how many multiples
   are in   r tower without counting each one?

5. Write   ltiplication equation that represents how
   many r   iples are in your multiple tower.

   _____ × _____ = _____

About Our Multiple Tower (page 2 of 2)

Answer these next questions without counting.

6. What is the 10th multiple? _____

7. What is the 20th multiple? _____

8. What is the 25th multiple? _____

9. How did you decide what the 20th multiple is?

10. Find each of the multiples above (10th, 20th, 25th) on your tower, and label them with a multiplication expression, such as 10×30.

11. What other landmark multiples can you find and label?

Arranging Juice Cans

NOTE Students solve story problems that involve finding factors.

 22

---

1. You have 24 juice cans. Show all of the ways you can arrange these cans into arrays. Draw the arrays.

2. List all the factors of 24.

---

3. Teyo has 25 juice cans. Show all of the ways he can arrange his cans into arrays. Draw the arrays.

4. List all the factors of 25.

---

5. Karina says, "25 has more factors than 24 because 25 is greater than 24." Do you agree or disagree with Karina? Explain.

Name _____   Date _____

Practice with Multiplication Cards 3

NOTE Students are working on the multiplication combinations (facts) to 12 × 12. Help your child with this practice.

SMH 33–34

1. Which multiplication combinations are you practicing?

_____

_____

_____

2. Write two multiplication combinations that are hard for you, and explain what helps you remember them.

Multiplication combination: _____

What helps me: _____

_____

_____

Multiplication combination: _____

What helps me: _____

_____

_____

Multiplying by Multiples of 10: What Happens? (page 2 of 2)

Now answer the following questions.

4. What do you notice about your solutions to the problems on page 42? In each set, how are your answers related?

5. Choose one of the sets of problems from page 42, and use cubes or a picture or diagram to show your thinking.

6. Try solving this problem:

$3 \times 400 =$

How is your answer to this problem different from your answer to 3×40? Why do you think that is?

NOTE Students practice solving multiplication and division problems.

SMH **36**

Kayla's Multiple Tower

The picture shows part of Kayla's multiple tower.

1. What number did Kayla count [by]? How do you know?

2. How many num[bers are in K]ayla's tower so far? How do you [know?]

3. Write a m[ultiplic]ation equation that represents how ma[ny nu]mbers are in Kayla's multiple tower.

   _____ × _____ = _____

4. Wha[t is th]e 10th multiple in Kayla's tower?

5. Supp[os]e that Kayla adds more multiples to her tower.
   a. [Wh]at would be the 20th multiple in her tower? [H]ow do you know?

   b. [W]hat would be the 25th multiple in her tower? [H]ow do you know?

On[go]ing Review

6. [Wh]ich of these numbers is not on Kayla's [mul]tiple tower?

   [A.] 9   **B.** 18   **C.** 72   **D.** 90

Counting Around the Class 2

NOTE Students find the multiples of a given number and solve multiplication problems.

SMH 25

1. Ms. Garcia's class counted by 25s. The first person said 25, the second person said 50, and the third said 75.

   How many people counted to get to 400? _____
   How do you know?

2. Mr. Wilson's class counted by 20s. The first person said 20, the second person said 40, and the third said 60.

   How many people counted to get to 400? _____
   How do you know?

3. Ms. Kleinman's class counted by 40s. The first person said 40, the second person said 80, and the third person said 120.

   a. How many people counted to get to 400? _____
   How do you know?

   b. When Ms. Kleinman's class counted by 40s, did anyone say the number 300? _____
   How do you know?

Solving a Cluster Problem

Solve the three multiplication cluster problems. Then solve the final problem. Explain how you solved the final problem, including which equations from the cluster helped you.

NOTE Students practice solving clusters of familiar multiplication problems, which can help them solve a related problem with larger numbers.

SMH 39

1. Cluster: $7 \times 3 =$

$7 \times 30 =$

$7 \times 4 =$

2. Final problem: $\mathbf{7 \times 34} =$

3. How did you solve 7×34?

Leg Riddles

People have 2 legs.
Cats have 4 legs.
Spiders have 8 legs.

NOTE Students solve multiplication problems in story problem contexts.

1. There are 3 spiders, 2 cats, and 5 people in the house.
   How many legs are there altogether?

2. There are 28 legs, and they all belong to cats.
   How many cats are there?

3. There are 30 legs in the house.
   All of the legs belong to people,
   cats, and spiders. How many of
   each creature—people, cats, and
   spiders—might be in the house?

   There are many possible answers.
   How many can you find?

People	Cats	Spiders

Sunken Treasure

Solve the problems. Use another sheet of paper if you need to. Show equations, pictures, and diagrams. Decide what to do with any extras.

NOTE Students solve division problems in a real-world context.

SMH 50–52

1. These are gold coins found at the site of a shipwreck. If a scuba diver could carry 18 of these coins to the surface in one trip, how many trips would it take to carry 108 coins?

2. If a scuba diver could carry 36 coins to the surface in one trip, how many trips would it take to carry 108 coins?

3. If five scuba divers found a total of 108 coins and were allowed to share them equally, how many coins would each scuba diver get?

4. If the five scuba divers were allowed to share only half of the 108 coins, how many coins would they each get?

Polished Spiral Karin Kuhlmann

"Although the creation of fractals is bounded to strict mathematical rules, the results are always very inspiring." – **Karin Kuhlmann**

Investigations
IN NUMBER, DATA, AND SPACE®

Size, Shape, and Symmetry

Investigation 3

Investigation 4

Measurement Benchmarks

Use a ruler, a yardstick, and a meter stick to find objects that are about as long as these measurement units. Record what you find.

Centimeter	Inch	Foot
Example: the tip of my pencil		

Yard	Meter
	Example: the height of the wall from the floor to the board

Using Measurement Benchmarks and Measurement Tools

Object	Estimate	Actual Measurement
Length of my pencil		
Width of my pencil		
Height of my desk from the floor		
Length of my notebook		
Width of the classroom window		
My teacher's height		

Size, Shape, and Symmetry

Perimeter Problems (page 1 of 2)

1. Estimate, and then find the perimeter of the objects listed below. Choose your own objects for the blank spaces.

Object	Unit of Measure (inches, feet, yards, centimeters, or meters)	Estimate	Actual Measurement
your classroom door			
your teacher's desk			
the board			

Perimeter Problems (page 2 of 2)

2. Choose one of your perimeter measurements. Estimate and measure it again using another unit.

3. Explain why the two measurements of the same perimeter are different.

Size, Shape, and Symmetry

Mapping 100 Feet

1. What tools did you use to map a path of 100 feet?

2. Draw your path.

3. What was the most challenging part of mapping out 100 feet?

Explaining Measurement Differences

1. Record all of the measurements your class found for the length of the classroom.

2. What is one of the smallest measurements? _____

3. Why did some people get smaller measurements?

4. What is one of the largest measurements? _____

5. Why did some people get larger measurements?

Directions for Making a Design

Work in pairs to make a symmetrical design.

1. Make a horizontal line of symmetry across the center of M23, Triangle Paper. One side will be Player 1's side; the other will be Player 2's side. Work only on your own side of the line.

2. Player 1 places a shape on the triangle paper, touching the line of symmetry on one side.

3. Player 2 puts the same kind of shape in the mirror-image position on the other side of the line.

4. Player 2 places a new shape on the paper. The shape must touch either the line of symmetry or at least one corner or side of a shape already placed.

5. Player 1 puts a shape in the mirror-image position of Player 2's shape.

6. Continue, until 12 shapes have been placed in all.

7. Set the first design to the side and start a new design on a separate sheet of Triangle Paper, following steps 1–6.

8. After you finish the second design, each player colors one of the designs. Use colors that match the Power Polygon piece.

Measuring Area with Triangles

Using the triangle piece, determine the area of each of the designs that you made. How many triangles does it take to cover the design?

1. Look at your first design. What is its area? _____

Explain how you determined its area.

2. Look at your second design. What is its area? _____

Explain how you determined its area.

Polished Spiral Karin Kuhlmann

"Although the creation of fractals is bounded to strict mathematical rules, the results are always very inspiring." – **Karin Kuhlmann**

Investigations

IN NUMBER, DATA, AND SPACE®

Landmarks and Large Numbers

Division Practice

Solve each division problem below. Then write the related multiplication combination.

NOTE Students review division problems that are related to the multiplication combinations they know.

 35

Division Problem	Multiplication Combination
1. $54 \div 9 =$ _____	_____ $\times$ _____ = _____
2. $55 \div 5 =$ _____	_____ $\times$ _____ = _____
3. $56 \div 8 =$ _____	_____ $\times$ _____ = _____
4. $84 \div 12 =$ _____	_____ $\times$ _____ = _____
5. $63 \div 9 =$ _____	_____ $\times$ _____ = _____
6. $96 \div 8 =$ _____	_____ $\times$ _____ = _____
7. $72 \div 9 =$ _____	_____ $\times$ _____ = _____
8. $64 \div 8 =$ _____	_____ $\times$ _____ = _____
9. $8\overline{)32}$	_____ $\times$ _____ = _____
10. $11\overline{)110}$	_____ $\times$ _____ = _____

Story Problems About 1,000

Solve the following problems and show your solutions.

> **NOTE** Students have been solving problems about how far numbers are from 1,000. In this homework, students solve these problems in a story context.
>
> **SMH** 11–12

1. Lily borrowed a new book from the library. At 1,000 pages, it is the longest book she has ever tried to read. In the first week, she read 89 pages. How many more pages does she have to read to reach the end?

2. In the next week, Lily read 450 more pages. How many pages does she have to read to reach the end?

3. By the end of 3 weeks, Lily read 932 pages altogether. How many pages does she have left to finish the book?

Multiplication Problems

Solve each of the problems below.
Show your thinking.

NOTE Students practice solving multiplication problems.

SMH 40, 41, 42

1. $27 \times 5 = $ _____

2. $43 \times 4 = $ _____

3. $6 \times 29 = $ _____

4. $34 \times 5 = $ _____

5. $30 \times 26 = $ _____

6. $12 \times 51 = $ _____

Ongoing Review

7. $14 \times 32 = $ _____

A. 160   **B.** 328   **C.** 334   **D.** 448

The Jones Family's Trip

How Many Miles?

Solve these problems about the Jones family's car trip. Show your solutions so that someone else can understand how you solved the problem.

1. In the first week of their trip, the Jones family drove 427 miles from their home in Ohio to Mammoth Cave in Kentucky. After their visit there, they drove 733 miles to Virginia Beach. How many miles did they drive altogether?

2. In the second week, the Jones family drove 270 miles from Virginia Beach to Philadelphia, Pennsylvania, to see the Liberty Bell. From Philadelphia, they drove to New York City, which is 96 miles away. How many miles did they drive altogether from Virginia Beach to New York City?

3. In the third week, the Jones family went to two more places in New York state. They drove 259 miles to see the Harriet Tubman House in Auburn, New York, and then 138 more miles to see Niagara Falls. Then it was time to go home, which was 235 miles away from Niagara Falls. How many miles did the Jones family drive in the third week of their trip?

Count Your Change Carefully

NOTE Students practice subtraction in the context of money and receiving change.

SMH 13–15

Complete this chart.

Item	Cost of Item	Amount Given to Clerk	Amount of Change
1. Ruler	$0.47	$1.00	
2. Sandwich	$3.18	$5.00	
3. Seeds	$1.55		$0.45
4. Socks	$2.74		$2.26
5. Shampoo		$1.00	$0.11
6. Apple		$5.00	$4.10
7. Stickers	$1.16	$10.00	
8. Magazine		$10.00	$6.35

Ongoing Review

9. 255 + _____ = 1,000

    A. 755   **B.** 750   **C.** 745   **D.** 705

Addition Starter Problems (page 1 of 2)

In Problems 1–6, solve all three starter problems. Then choose one of the starter problems and use it to solve the final problem. Put a star next to the starter problem that you used and show how you finished the problem.

1. 300 + 500 = _____   315 + 500 = _____   315 + 5 = _____

   Choose one of the starter problems above and use it to solve this problem:

   315 + 566 =

2. 288 + 400 = _____   200 + 400 = _____   300 + 450 = _____

   Choose one of the starter problems above and use it to solve this problem:

   288 + 456 =

3. 597 + 300 = _____   600 + 375 = _____   600 + 372 = _____

   Choose one of the starter problems above and use it to solve this problem:

   597 + 375 =

Addition Starter Problems (page 2 of 2)

4. $9.94 + $5.00 = ___ $9.00 + $5.00 = ___ $0.94 + $0.06 = ___

Choose one of the starter problems above and use it to solve
this problem:

$9.94 + $5.16 =

5. 500 + 300 + 200 = ___   532 + 300 + 200 = ___
530 + 370 = ___

Choose one of the starter problems above and use it to solve
this problem:

1,532
2,371
+ 212
---

6. 785 + 400 = ___   800 + 428 = ___   785 + 15 = ___

Choose one of the starter problems above and use it to solve
this problem:

785 + 428 =

Related Problems About Multiplying Groups of 10

NOTE Students practice solving multiplication problems and explain any patterns about multiplying groups of 10 that they notice in each pair of problems.

SMH 37–38

Solve each pair of multiplication problems below.

1. 8×6 = _____

8×60 = _____

2. 7×7 = _____

7×70 = _____

3. 9×7 = _____

90×7 = _____

4. 12×8 = _____

120×8 = _____

5. 15×5 = _____

15×50 = _____

6. 6×13 = _____

60×13 = _____

7. 11×4 = _____

11×40 = _____

8. 60×5 = _____

600×5 = _____

Ongoing Review

9. Which is 400 less than 866?

A. 862   **B.** 826   **C.** 466   **D.** 422

How Do You Solve an Addition Problem?

NOTE Students practice solving addition problems. Share with your child how you would solve the problem.

 SMH 8–10

To the student:

1. Solve this problem and show your solution:

   $299 + 156 = $ _____

To the adult:

2. How would you solve this problem? Please record your solution. (If you solved the problem mentally, explain what you did.)

   $$\begin{array}{r} 299 \\ +156 \\ \hline \end{array}$$

3. Is this the way you were taught to solve addition problems when you were in school? If not, solve it the way you were taught.

   $$\begin{array}{r} 299 \\ +156 \\ \hline \end{array}$$

Two Different Solutions

1. Solve this problem. Show your solution, using clear and concise notation.

$$145 + 226 = \underline{\hspace{3cm}}$$

Now look carefully at these two different solutions for the same problem. Answer the questions below.

Solution 1

```
  145
+226
─────
  300
   60
+  11
─────
  371
```

Solution 2

```
   1
  145
+226
─────
  371
```

2. How would you explain to someone else how Solution 1 works? (Where does the 60 come from? Where does the 11 come from?)

3. How would you explain to someone else how Solution 2 works? (Where does the 1 above the 4 in 145 come from?)

Solving an Addition Problem in Two Ways

NOTE Students practice strategies for addition by solving a problem in two ways.

SMH 8–9

1. Solve this problem in two different ways. Be sure to show how you got your answer.

431 + 799 = _____

Here is the first way I solved it:

Here is the second way I solved it:

Ongoing Review

2. Which of the following is true?

A. 11 + 880 > 1,000

C. 733 + 218 > 1,000

B. 642 + 419 > 1,000

D. 82 + 904 > 1,000

Close to 1,000 Recording Sheet

Game 1   **Score**

Round 1: ____ ____ ____ + ____ ____ ____ = ____   ____

Round 2: ____ ____ ____ + ____ ____ ____ = ____   ____

Round 3: ____ ____ ____ + ____ ____ ____ = ____   ____

Round 4: ____ ____ ____ + ____ ____ ____ = ____   ____

Round 5: ____ ____ ____ + ____ ____ ____ = ____   ____

Final Score ____

Game 2   **Score**

Round 1: ____ ____ ____ + ____ ____ ____ = ____   ____

Round 2: ____ ____ ____ + ____ ____ ____ = ____   ____

Round 3: ____ ____ ____ + ____ ____ ____ = ____   ____

Round 4: ____ ____ ____ + ____ ____ ____ = ____   ____

Round 5: ____ ____ ____ + ____ ____ ____ = ____   ____

Final Score ____

Apple Orchard

Solve the story problems below. Show your work and your equations.

NOTE Students practice solving multiplication and division problems in story problem contexts.

SMH 45

1. At an apple orchard, small bags contain 7 apples. Alexa and her family bought 91 apples for a party. How many small bags did they buy?

2. Large bags hold 14 apples. When a fourth-grade class went apple picking, they filled 9 large bags. How many apples did they pick?

3. Savanna and her three brothers picked 55 apples. They shared the apples equally among the four of them. How many apples did each child get? Were there any apples left over?

Related Problems About Doubling and Halving

NOTE Students practice solving multiplication problems. Ask your child to explain any patterns he or she notices in each set of problems.

SMH 43

Solve each set of multiplication problems below.

1. 4×7 = _____

   8×7 = _____

   8×14 = _____

2. 6×9 = _____

   12×9 = _____

   6×18 = _____

3. 3×11 = _____

   6×11 = _____

   6×22 = _____

4. 5×8 = _____

   10×8 = _____

   20×8 = _____

5. 3×15 = _____

   3×30 = _____

   6×15 = _____

6. 32×4 = _____

   16×8 = _____

   8×8 = _____

Choose Wisely

Add the number in the first box to each of the other two numbers. Draw the path that gets you closest to 1,000.

NOTE Students practice adding numbers whose total is near 1,000.

SMH 8–9

Example:

I chose 691 because 310 + 691 = 1,001, but 310 + 670 = 980.

1.

$$\begin{array}{r} 780 \\ +214 \\ \hline 994 \end{array} \qquad \begin{array}{r} 790 \\ +214 \\ \hline 1004 \end{array}$$

780

214

790

2.

515

480

522

$$\begin{array}{r} 480 \\ +515 \\ \hline 995 \end{array}$$

$$\begin{array}{r} 522 \\ +480 \\ \hline 1002 \end{array}$$

3.

545

555

555

$$\begin{array}{r} 555 \\ +545 \\ \hline 1100 \end{array} \qquad \begin{array}{r} 555 \\ +555 \\ \hline 1110 \end{array}$$

4.

199

807

203

$$\begin{array}{r} 800 \\ +199 \\ \hline 1006 \end{array} \qquad \begin{array}{r} 807 \\ +203 \\ \hline 1010 \end{array}$$

Ongoing Review

5. Which number could be read as "thirteen hundred"?

A. 130   **B.** 1,003   **C.** 1,013   **D.** 1,300

Session 3.1

How Many 10s Are in 10,000?

From your work on the 10,000 chart, you know that:

There are ten 1,000s in 10,000.
There are one hundred 100s in 10,000.

How would you explain to a third-grade student
how many 10s there are in 10,000?

Write your explanation on a separate sheet of paper. You
may write it as a letter to a third-grade student if you wish.
You may also include any pictures or equations that you
think will help make your explanation clearer.

Pick a Number

The first and last numbers of some 100 charts are shown. Write another number that belongs on each chart.

NOTE Students practice finding a number on 100 charts.

SMH 6

1.

| 1,201 |
| _____ |
| 1,300 |

2.

| 2,401 |
| _____ |
| 2,500 |

3.

| 3,501 |
| _____ |
| 3,600 |

4.

| 5,901 |
| _____ |
| 6,000 |

5.

| 7,701 |
| _____ |
| 7,800 |

6.

| 9,001 |
| _____ |
| 9,100 |

Ongoing Review

7. Which number is between 4,009 and 4,156?

A. 4,005   **B.** 4,056   **C.** 4,160   **D.** 4,500

All About the Number (page 1 of 2)

Answer the following questions about the number 4,736.

NOTE Students are making a 10,000 chart to help them understand how our number system is constructed and to see important relationships within the number system. This homework focuses on these relationships, such as place value and "landmark numbers" (multiples of 10 and 100).

SMH 6

1. Is 4,736 closer to 4,000 or 5,000? How do you know?

2. Choose a landmark number that is close to 4,736.

3. Does 4,736 come before or after that landmark number?

4. What is 300 more than 4,736?

All About the Number (page 2 of 2)

5. What is 50 less than 4,736?

6. If I put 4,736 marbles into groups of 100, how many groups would I have? Show how you figured it out.

7. If I put 4,736 marbles into groups of 10, how many groups would I have? Show how you figured it out.

Cities Around the U.S.

Landmarks and Large Numbers

City to City: How Many Miles?

This table shows driving distances between various U.S. cities.

	Boston, MA	Washington, D.C.	Orlando, FL	Nashville, TN	Minneapolis, MN	Dallas, TX	Denver, CO	Los Angeles, CA	Seattle, WA
Seattle, WA	3,046	2,764	3,135	2,450	1,658	2,202	1,332	1,138	0
Los Angeles, CA	2,984	2,655	2,513	2,006	1,928	1,434	1,018	0	1,138
Denver, CO	1,970	1,671	1,842	1,157	915	879	0	1,018	1,332
Dallas, TX	1,816	1,329	1,090	664	990	0	879	1,434	2,202
Minneapolis, MN	1,389	1,107	1,568	884	0	990	915	1,928	1,685
Nashville, TN	1,154	666	688	0	884	664	1,157	2,006	2,450
Orlando, FL	1,300	852	0	688	1,568	1,090	1,842	2,513	3,135
Washington, D.C.	446	0	852	666	1,107	1,329	1,671	2,655	2,764
Boston, MA	0	446	1,300	1,154	1,389	1,816	1,970	2,984	3,046

Planning a Road Trip

From your map of the United States, choose at least 3 cities for your complete road trip. Use the table on page 46 to find the distance between the cities on your trip. Make an addition problem about how far you will travel on your trip, and solve the problem. Show your solution.

Trip 1

1. Where will you start your trip?   _____

2. What city (or cities) will you visit?   _____

3. Where will you finish your trip?   _____

4. How many miles is your road trip altogether?
   Show how you figured it out.

Trip 2

5. Where will you start your trip?   _____

6. What city (or cities) will you visit?   _____

7. Where will you finish your trip?   _____

8. How many miles is your road trip altogether?
   Show how you figured it out.

Changing Place Values

Solve each problem, showing your solutions clearly. Then write which place value(s) in the first number changed.

NOTE Students add and subtract 10s, 100s, and 1,000s to and from multi-digit numbers and determine which place values have changed.

SMH 6

1. $6,652 + 600 + 1,000 =$

Which place value(s) changed? _____

2. $3,719 - 2,000 + 50 =$

Which place value(s) changed? _____

3. $9,006 - 800 + 300 =$

Which place value(s) changed? _____

Ongoing Review

4. How many 1,000s are in 8,008?

   A. 8   **B.** 80   **C.** 800   **D.** 8,000

Broken Calculator

Find five solutions to each of these problems.

NOTE Students practice building flexibility with addition, subtraction, multiplication, and division.

1. I want to make 35 by using my calculator, but the 3 key and the 5 key are broken. How can I use my calculator to do this task?

2. I want to make 100 by using my calculator, but the 0 key and the + key are broken. How can I use my calculator to do this task?

3. I want to make 48 by using my calculator, but the 4 key and the 8 key are broken. How can I use my calculator to do this task?

4. I want to make 99 by using my calculator, but the 9 key, the + key, and the − key are broken. How can I use my calculator to do this task?

5. I want to make 500 by using my calculator, but the 5 key, the + key, and the − key are broken. How can I use my calculator to do this task?

What's for Lunch?

Look at the menu below and imagine that you are ordering lunch for yourself and a friend. Choose at least 5 things. (Two could be drinks.) Write an addition problem about how much this lunch will cost and solve the problem. Show your solution.

NOTE Students practice adding amounts of money.

SMH 8–9

Joe's Cafe

Tacos	$5.38	**Drinks:**	
Hamburger	$4.59	Lemonade	$1.52
Chicken Soup	$2.06	Orange Juice	$1.79
Greek Salad	$4.79	Milk	$1.25
Tuna Sandwich	$3.43	Spring Water	$1.52
Peanut Butter and			
Jelly Sandwich	$3.65		
Egg Rolls	$2.26		
French Fries	$1.98		

1. What will you order for lunch?

2. How much will your lunch cost?

Subtraction Problems

Solve each subtraction problem.
Show your work clearly.

NOTE Students practice solving subtraction problems.

SMH 13–15

1. $1,200 - 635 =$ _____

2. $884 - 591 =$ _____

3. 711
      -258
      ——

Ongoing Review

4. Which of the following is true?

    A. $618 - 117 < 500$ **C.** $956 - 455 > 500$

    B. $733 - 234 > 500$ **D.** $876 - 375 < 500$

Close to 1,300

Read the story below and answer the questions.

NOTE Students solve addition problems to create a sum of 1,300.

SMH 8–9

Robert and Leslie are playing a game they made up called *Close to 1,300*. The object of the game, as in *Close to 1,000,* is to make two numbers that total as close to 1,300 as possible.

1. Robert made this combination:

   937 + 365

   What is Robert's total? _____

2. Leslie made this combination:

   424 + 856

   What is Leslie's total? _____

3. Who is closer to 1,300? _____

4. What is each person's score? (Remember that the score is the difference between the total and 1,300.)

   Robert's score: _____   Leslie's score: _____

Solving Subtraction Problems (page 1 of 2)

Solve each problem and show your solution.

1. $631 - 268 = $ _____

2. 704
     −551

3. Jenna has 826 stamps in her collection. Ricardo has
637 stamps in his collection. How many more stamps
does Jenna have?

Solving Subtraction Problems (page 2 of 2)

4. The Diamond Egg Farm had 1,321 chickens. Last month they sold 663 of them to another farm. How many chickens do they have left?

5. In 1985, the population of West Littlebury was 1,877 people. In 2005, the population was 2,391 people. By how many people did the population of West Littlebury increase from 1985 to 2005?

6. $4,495 - 2,504 =$ _____

What's the Story?

Write a story to go with each problem. Then solve the problem and show your solution.

1.   947
        −182

2. 1,253 − 940 = _____

3. 714 − 399 = _____

What Should We Do with the Extras?

NOTE Students practice solving division problems and interpreting remainders in story problem contexts.

SMH 48, 49

Solve the problems below. Make sure that you keep track of all the steps you take. Write equations to show the steps of your solution.

1. Joey and his aunt picked 96 apples at the orchard. They plan to put them in bags of 8 apples each. How many bags of apples can they fill?

   Division equation: ___96___ ÷ ___8___ = _____   Answer: _____ bags

2. Five friends earned $72 from washing cars. They want to share the money equally among the five of them. How much money will each of the friends receive?

   Division equation: _____ ÷ _____ = _____   Answer: _____

3. Glue sticks come in packages of five. The art teacher at the Glendale School needs 72 glue sticks in her classroom. How many packages of glue sticks will she need to buy?

   Division equation: _____ ÷ _____ = _____   Answer: _____

Daily Practice

Events at the Community Center

Many events are held at the community center. Here are some events and the attendance at these events.

NOTE Students solve addition and subtraction problems in a story context.

SMH **8–9, 13–15**

Event	Attendance
Science Fair	368
Basketball Tournament	741
Book Fair	555
Swim Meet	496
Rock Concert	1,152
Homecoming Dance	783

1. What was the total attendance of the science fair and the rock concert?

2. Which event had more people in attendance, the homecoming dance or the swim meet? How many more?

3. a. Which 3 events had the highest attendance?

b. What was the total attendance at those 3 events?

© Pearson Education 4

The U.S. Algorithm (page 1 of 2)

Use the U.S. algorithm for subtraction to solve the following problems. (Then solve the problems using a different strategy to make sure your final answer is correct.)

In Problems 1 and 2, the steps of the U.S. algorithm are shown. Fill in the blanks with the correct numbers.

1.

$$\begin{array}{r} 757 \\ -428 \\ \hline \end{array}$$

$$\begin{array}{r} 700 \quad + \quad 50 \quad + \quad 7 \\ -(400 \quad + \quad 20 \quad + \quad 8) \\ \hline \end{array}$$

$$\begin{array}{r} ^4_1 \\ 7\cancel{5}7 \\ -428 \\ \hline \end{array}$$

$$\begin{array}{r} 700 \quad + \quad \underline{} \quad + \quad \underline{} \\ -(400 \quad + \quad 20 \quad + \quad 8) \\ \hline \underline{} \quad + \quad \underline{} \quad + \quad \underline{} \end{array}$$

2.

$$\begin{array}{r} 526 \\ -188 \\ \hline \end{array}$$

$$\begin{array}{r} 500 \quad + \quad 20 \quad + \quad 6 \\ -(100 \quad + \quad 80 \quad + \quad 8) \\ \hline \end{array}$$

$$\begin{array}{r} ^4{}^1{}_1 \\ \cancel{5}\cancel{2}\cancel{6} \\ -188 \\ \hline \end{array}$$

$$\begin{array}{r} \underline{} \quad + \quad \underline{} \quad + \quad \underline{} \\ -(100 \quad + \quad 80 \quad + \quad 8) \\ \hline \underline{} \quad + \quad \underline{} \quad + \quad \underline{} \end{array}$$

© Pearson Education 4

The U.S. Algorithm (page 2 of 2)

For Problems 3 and 4, use the U.S. algorithm for subtraction to solve each problem. Also, write the correct numbers in the blanks, showing how you broke apart the original numbers.

3. $\begin{array}{r} 361 \\ -143 \end{array}$ $\begin{array}{r} 300 \quad + \quad 60 \quad + \quad 1 \\ -(100 \quad + \quad 40 \quad + \quad 3) \end{array}$

$\begin{array}{r} 361 \\ -143 \end{array}$ $\begin{array}{r} \underline{\quad} + \underline{\quad} + \underline{\quad} \\ -(\underline{\quad} + \underline{\quad} + \underline{\quad}) \end{array}$

4. $\begin{array}{r} 844 \\ -757 \end{array}$ $\begin{array}{r} 800 \quad + \quad 40 \quad + \quad 4 \\ -(700 \quad + \quad 50 \quad + \quad 7) \end{array}$

$\begin{array}{r} 844 \\ -757 \end{array}$ $\begin{array}{r} \underline{\quad} + \underline{\quad} + \underline{\quad} \\ -(\underline{\quad} + \underline{\quad} + \underline{\quad}) \end{array}$

Using the U.S. Algorithm

Use the U.S. algorithm for subtraction to solve each problem. Also, write the correct numbers in the blanks, showing how you broke apart the original numbers.

NOTE Students practice using the U.S. algorithm for subtraction by breaking apart the numbers by place and regrouping when necessary. They also practice the standard notation for this algorithm.

1. 498
     − 279

400	+	90	+	8
− (200	+	70	+	9)

     498
   − 279

____	+	____	+	____
− (____	+	____	+	____)

2. 525
     − 164

500	+	20	+	5
− (100	+	60	+	4)

     525
   − 164

____	+	____	+	____
− (____	+	____	+	____)

Subtraction Starter Problems

In each set of problems below, solve all three starter problems. Then choose one of the starter problems, and use it to solve the final problem. Put a star next to the starter problem that you used, and show how you finished the problem.

1. $97 - 40 =$ _____ $97 - 30 =$ _____ $100 - 39 =$ _____

Choose one of the starter problems above and use it to solve this problem:

$97 - 39 =$

2. $150 - 80 =$ _____ $150 - 75 =$ _____ $78 + 22 =$ _____

Choose one of the starter problems above and use it to solve this problem:

$150 - 78 =$

3. $413 - 300 =$ _____ $413 - 200 =$ _____ $295 + 5 =$ _____

Choose one of the starter problems above and use it to solve this problem:

$413 - 295 =$

Which Is Farther?
How Much Farther? (page 1 of 2)

For each pair of cities below, look at the information on page 46 and write the distance between them. Then, circle the distance that is farther, answer the question "How much farther?", and show your solution.

1. Which is farther: Orlando to Minneapolis?

_____
(Write the distance here.)

or

Orlando to Denver?

_____
(Write the distance here.)

How much farther?

2. Which is farther: Dallas to Seattle?

_____
(Write the distance here.)

or

Dallas to Boston?

_____
(Write the distance here.)

How much farther?

3. Which is farther: Los Angeles to Washington, D.C.?

_____
(Write the distance here.)

or

Los Angeles to Minneapolis?

_____
(Write the distance here.)

How much farther?

Landmarks and Large Numbers

Which Is Farther?
How Much Farther? (page 2 of 2)

Look at the chart on page 46. Choose two cities and write the distance between them.

4. Which is farther: _____ to _____ ? _____
  (city)   (city)   (Write the distance here.)

   or

   _____ to _____ ? _____
   (city)   (city)   (Write the distance here.)

   How much farther?

5. Which is farther: _____ to _____ ? _____
  (city)   (city)   (Write the distance here.)

   or

   _____ to _____ ? _____
   (city)   (city)   (Write the distance here.)

   How much farther?

6. Which is farther: _____ to _____ ? _____
  (city)   (city)   (Write the distance here.)

   or

   _____ to _____ ? _____
   (city)   (city)   (Write the distance here.)

   How much farther?

Money Problems (page 1 of 2)

Solve the problems below and show your solutions.

1. Ms. Chung went to the grocery store with $25.00 in her wallet. When she was finished shopping, she had $8.37. How much did the groceries cost?

2. Emily is saving to buy a desk and chair for her room. The desk costs $69.50. The chair costs $52.89. Emily has saved $39.40 so far. How much more does she need to save?

3. $262.51
   −$121.95
   _____

Money Problems (page 2 of 2)

4. Mr. Ortega took Ruben out for ice cream. Their ice cream cones cost $2.59 each. Mr. Ortega paid for both ice cream cones with a $10.00 bill. How much change did he receive?

5. Both John's and Eva's classes are collecting cans for recycling to raise money for a class trip. John's class has earned $46.30. Eva's class has earned $37.85. How much more money has John's class earned?

6. $30.52 + $18.78 + $43.22 = _____

More Subtraction Starter Problems

NOTE Students solve subtraction problems using different starts.

SMH 13–15

In each set of problems below, solve all three starter problems. Then choose one of the starter problems, and use it to solve the final problem. Put a star next to the starter problem that you used and show how you finished the solution.

1. $300 - 100 =$ _____ $363 - 100 =$ _____ $363 - 130 =$ _____

Choose one of the starter problems above and use it to solve this problem:

$363 - 129 =$

2. $805 - 600 =$ _____ $805 - 700 =$ _____ $694 + 6 =$ _____

Choose one of the starter problems above and use it to solve this problem:

$805 - 694 =$

Ongoing Review

3. Which expression is closest to 1,300?

A. $685 + 735$ **C.** $653 + 612$

B. $903 + 405$ **D.** $1,234 + 142$

Subtraction Practice

Use the U.S. algorithm for subtraction to solve each problem. Also, write the correct numbers in the blanks, showing how you broke apart the original numbers.

NOTE Students practice using the U.S. algorithm for subtraction by breaking apart the numbers by place and regrouping when necessary. They also practice the standard notation for this algorithm.

1. $\begin{array}{r} 781 \\ -593 \\ \hline \end{array}$ $\begin{array}{r} 700 \quad + \quad 80 \quad + \quad 1 \\ -(500 \quad + \quad 90 \quad + \quad 3) \\ \hline \end{array}$

    $\begin{array}{r} 781 \\ -593 \\ \hline \end{array}$ $\begin{array}{r} \underline{\quad} \quad + \quad \underline{\quad} \quad + \quad \underline{\quad} \\ -(\underline{\quad} \quad + \quad \underline{\quad} \quad + \quad \underline{\quad}) \\ \hline \end{array}$

2. $\begin{array}{r} 933 \\ -647 \\ \hline \end{array}$ $\begin{array}{r} 900 \quad + \quad 30 \quad + \quad 3 \\ -(600 \quad + \quad 40 \quad + \quad 7) \\ \hline \end{array}$

    $\begin{array}{r} 933 \\ -647 \\ \hline \end{array}$ $\begin{array}{r} \underline{\quad} \quad + \quad \underline{\quad} \quad + \quad \underline{\quad} \\ -(\underline{\quad} \quad + \quad \underline{\quad} \quad + \quad \underline{\quad}) \\ \hline \end{array}$

Mystery Tower (page 1 of 2)

The picture shows the top part of Richard's multiple tower. Answer these questions about his tower.

NOTE Students practice solving multiplication and division problems.

SMH 36

1. What number did Richard count by? How do you know?

192

176

160

144

128

2. How many numbers are in Richard's tower so far? How do you know?

3. Write a multiplication equation that represents how many numbers are in Richard's multiple tower.

   _____ × _____ = _____

Mystery Tower (page 2 of 2)

4. What is the 10th multiple in Richard's tower?

5. Imagine that Richard adds more multiples to his tower.

   a. What would be the 20th multiple in his tower?
   How do you know?

   b. What would be the 25th multiple in his tower?
   How do you know?

Ongoing Review

6. 8,350 − 400 + 60 = _____

   A. 8,110   **B.** 8,100   **C.** 8,010   **D.** 8,001

Addition and Subtraction Practice

Solve the problems below and show your solutions.

NOTE Students practice solving both addition and subtraction problems.

SMH **8–9, 13–15**

1. The U.S. Olympic Soccer Team played in several cities around the United States. They played their first game in Los Angeles, and then flew to Denver, which is 1,018 miles away. After the Denver game, they flew to Dallas, which is 879 miles from Denver. How many miles has the team traveled?

2. A new player joined the team. She flew straight from Los Angeles to Dallas, which is 1,434 miles away. How many fewer miles did she travel than the team?

Daily Practice

Shark Attack! (page 1 of 2)

Shown below are sharks found around the world
and their typical weights, in pounds.

NOTE Students practice
solving both addition and
subtraction problems.

 8–9, 11–12, 13,
14, 15

Great White
2,600 pounds

Tiger
1,125 pounds

Sandbar
130 pounds

Hammerhead
500 pounds

Greenland
1,705 pounds

Answer the following questions, using the information
shown above. Try to do some of the problems mentally.
Show your written work on another sheet of paper.

1. A fisherman caught a hammerhead shark and a
sandbar shark. What is the combined weight?

2. Some newspapers reported that a great white shark
with a weight of 7,032 pounds was caught off the
coast of Cuba in 1945. Some scientists, however, think
that the story is just a fish tale. What is the difference
between the weight of the legendary Cuban great
white shark and the weight of a typical great
white shark?

Shark Attack! (page 2 of 2)

3. A great white shark can eat as much as 400 pounds in one meal! If a great white shark has a 352-pound dinner, what does the shark weigh immediately after finishing its meal?

4. Three 180-pound men are fishing for sharks. Which of these is a heavier load on their boat:

3 men, a Greenland shark, and a sandbar shark?

or

3 men, 2 hammerhead sharks, and a tiger shark?

How did you get your answer?

Polished Spiral Karin Kuhlmann

"Although the creation of fractals is bounded to strict mathematical rules, the results are always very inspiring." – **Karin Kuhlmann**

Investigations
IN NUMBER, DATA, AND SPACE®

Student Activity Book

Fraction Cards and Decimal Squares

UNIT 6

Fraction Cards and Decimal Squares

Investigation 3

4 × 6 Rectangles

Solve Two Ways, Addition

Solve this problem in two different ways.
Be sure to show how you got your answer.

NOTE Students practice strategies for solving addition problems in two different ways.

SMH 8–9

$293 + 851 =$ _____

Here is the first way I solved it:

Here is the second way I solved it:

Ongoing Review

$924 + 150 =$ _____

A. 1,024   **B.** 1,074   **C.** 1,390   **D.** 1,740

Fraction Cards and Decimal Squares   **Homework**

Halves, Fourths, and Eighths

Shade in each fraction on one of the rectangles.
Label the fraction on each rectangle.

NOTE Students represent fractions on a 4 × 6 rectangle.

SMH **53, 54, 56**

$\dfrac{1}{4}$ $\dfrac{1}{2}$ $\dfrac{2}{2}$ $\dfrac{3}{4}$ $\dfrac{1}{8}$ $\dfrac{7}{8}$

4

Fraction Cards and Decimal Squares

Parts of Rectangles

What fraction of the rectangle is shaded?
Write the fraction next to each figure.

NOTE Students identify fractional parts of a rectangle.

 SMH 56–57

1. _____

2. _____

3. _____

4. _____

5. _____

6. _____

7. _____

8. _____

9. _____

10. _____

Story Problems About 24 (page 1 of 2)

Solve these problems and show your solutions.

1. Ethan has 24 marbles. He gives $\frac{2}{8}$ of his collection to his sister Ruby. How many marbles does Ruby get?

2. Ruby has a collection of 24 toy cars. She gives $\frac{3}{4}$ of her collection to Ethan. How many toy cars does Ethan get?

Story Problems About 24 (page 2 of 2)

Solve these problems and show your solutions.

3. a. Ms. Ross's class has 24 students. $\frac{2}{3}$ of her students have brown hair. The rest have blonde hair. How many students have brown hair?

b. What fraction of the class has blonde hair and how many students is that?

4. a. Ms. Perez has a crate of 24 pieces of fruit. $\frac{1}{2}$ are oranges, $\frac{1}{4}$ are mangos, and $\frac{2}{8}$ are pineapples. How many oranges are there?

b. How many mangos are there?

c. How many pineapples are there?

Solve Two Ways, Subtraction

NOTE Students practice strategies for solving subtraction problems in two different ways.

SMH 13–15

Solve this problem in two different ways.
Be sure to show how you got your answer.

$745 - 328 =$ _____

Here is the first way I solved it:

Here is the second way I solved it:

Ongoing Review

$2,050 - 400 - 30 =$

A. 1,020   **B.** 1,520   **C.** 1,580   **D.** 1,620

Sharing 24 (page 1 of 2)

> **NOTE** Students find fractional parts of a group of objects.
>
> **SMH** 55

Solve these problems and explain your solutions.

Mia had 24 marbles.

1. Mia gave $\frac{1}{2}$ of her 24 marbles to Shana. How many did Shana get?

2. Mia gave $\frac{1}{3}$ of her 24 marbles to David. How many did David get?

Fraction Cards and Decimal Squares

Homework

Sharing 24 (page 2 of 2)

3. Mia gave $\frac{1}{6}$ of her 24 marbles to Yama. How many did Yama get?

4. Show each fraction on the 4 × 6 rectangle below. Label each piece.

5 × 12 Rectangles

Story Problems About a Class (page 1 of 2)

Solve each problem and show your solution clearly.

1. Renata's fourth-grade class has 28 students. $\frac{1}{2}$ of her class is on the soccer team. $\frac{1}{4}$ of her class takes karate classes.

   a. How many students are on the soccer team?

   b. How many students take karate?

2. Kenji's fourth-grade class has 32 students. $\frac{1}{2}$ of his class is in the school play. $\frac{1}{4}$ of his class is on the swim team.

   a. How many students are in the play?

   b. How many students are on the swim team?

Story Problems About a Class (page 2 of 2)

Solve each problem and show your solution clearly.

3. The school play includes 60 students. $\frac{3}{5}$ of the students are actors. The rest of the students work behind the scenes.

   a. How many students act in the play?

   b. How many students work behind the scenes?

4. Luisa has 24 students in her class. $\frac{3}{4}$ of the students speak Spanish as well as English. How many students speak both Spanish and English?

5. Nick's class has 30 students. $\frac{2}{5}$ of his class sings in the school chorus. How many students sing in the chorus?

Fractional Parts of Groups

Solve these problems and explain
your solutions.

NOTE Students identify fractional
parts of a group.

 55

1. Logan caught 16 butterflies this morning. By the
   evening, $\frac{1}{4}$ of the butterflies had flown away. How
   many butterflies remain?

2. Talisha collected pledges from 40 people for the
   charity race. $\frac{1}{8}$ of the people are family members.
   How many people who pledged are family members?

3. Paul hit 33 tennis balls during practice. He hit $\frac{1}{3}$ of them
   out of the tennis court. How many balls did he hit out
   of the court?

4. Maria read 90 books last school year. She read $\frac{2}{3}$
   of the books before spring break. How many books
   did she read before spring break last year?

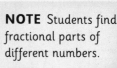

Finding Fractions of a Number

Solve these problems and show your solutions.

NOTE Students find fractional parts of different numbers.

 SMH 55

1. **a.** What is $\frac{1}{2}$ of 24?   **b.** What is $\frac{1}{3}$ of 24?   **c.** What is $\frac{1}{4}$ of 24?

2. **a.** What is $\frac{1}{2}$ of 30?   **b.** What is $\frac{1}{3}$ of 30?   **c.** What is $\frac{2}{3}$ of 30?

3. **a.** What is $\frac{1}{2}$ of 60?   **b.** What is $\frac{1}{3}$ of 60?   **c.** What is $\frac{1}{4}$ of 60?

4. Show with a diagram or picture why $\frac{1}{2}$ of 60 is not the same as $\frac{1}{2}$ of 24.

16

Unit 6

Addition and Subtraction Problems

NOTE Students practice solving addition and subtraction problems.

SMH **8–9, 13–15**

Solve the problems below. Show your solutions using clear and concise notation.

1. 738
     −680

2. 515
     − 472

3. 811 + 749 = _____

4. 1,234
     + 694

5. _____ + 349 = 1,250

6. 865 − _____ = 347

Show the Fraction

Use these rectangles to show the following fractions as clearly as you can. Explain your thinking about each one.

NOTE Students represent fractional parts of a rectangle.

 56–57

1. $\frac{5}{6}$

2. $\frac{3}{3}$

3. $\frac{4}{8}$

4. $\frac{2}{3}$

Adding Fractions (page 1 of 3)

Solve each problem and show your solution.

1. Alexa ate $\frac{1}{8}$ of a sandwich. Dwayne ate another $\frac{1}{8}$ of the same sandwich. Sara ate $\frac{1}{4}$ of the same sandwich.

   a. How much of the sandwich did Alexa, Dwayne, and Sara eat altogether?

   b. What fraction of the sandwich is left?

2. Ms. Russell has 24 students in her class. $\frac{3}{8}$ of the class went out for recess. $\frac{1}{4}$ went to the library. The rest stayed in the classroom.

   a. What fraction of the class was out of the classroom?

   b. How many students is that?

Adding Fractions (page 2 of 3)

Solve each problem and show your solution.

3. $\frac{1}{2} + \frac{3}{8} = $ _____

4. $\frac{1}{3} + \frac{1}{2} + \frac{2}{3} = $ _____

5. $\frac{1}{2} + \frac{3}{6} + \frac{4}{8} = $ _____

6. $\frac{5}{6} + \frac{1}{3} = $ _____

7. $\frac{3}{12} + \frac{1}{2} + \frac{1}{4} = $ _____

8. $\frac{1}{4} + \frac{3}{8} + \frac{1}{4} = $ _____

Adding Fractions (page 3 of 3)

Solve each problem and show your solution.

9. Leon bought a big bag of marbles. $\frac{1}{3}$ of them are blue. $\frac{1}{6}$ of them are red. The rest are yellow.

   a. What fraction of the marbles is yellow?

   b. There were 30 marbles in the bag. Arielle borrowed the blue and red marbles. How many marbles did she borrow?

10. Write fractions to show all the parts of this rectangle. Then write an equation that shows how all the fractional parts add up to 1.

_____ + _____ + _____ + _____ + _____ + _____ = 1

Combinations That Equal 1

Use these rectangles to find combinations of fractions that equal 1. Show the fractions on each rectangle and write the matching equation underneath.

_____ = 1

_____ = 1

_____ = 1

_____ = 1

_____ = 1

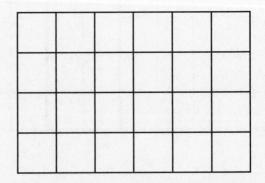

_____ = 1

10 × 10 Squares

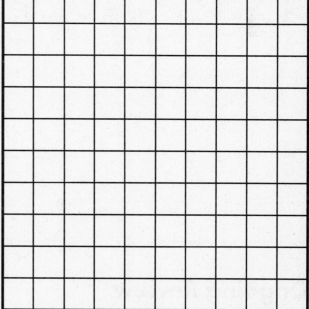

Sums of Fractions That Equal 1: True or False?

NOTE Students decide whether an equation involving fractions is true or false.

SMH 62

Is the equation correct? Circle TRUE or FALSE and show how you know.

1. $\frac{1}{3} + \frac{2}{3} = 1$ TRUE or FALSE

2. $\frac{4}{8} + \frac{3}{6} = 1$ TRUE or FALSE

3. $\frac{3}{6} + \frac{1}{3} = 1$ TRUE or FALSE

4. $\frac{2}{3} + \frac{3}{6} = 1$ TRUE or FALSE

Ongoing Review

5. Which picture does **not** show $\frac{1}{6}$ of a rectangle shaded?

A.   B.   C.   D.

Fraction Match-Ups

Draw a line connecting each diagram to its matching fraction.

NOTE Students have been drawing diagrams to represent fractions. Ask students whether they can think of a different way to write the fraction for the diagrams in Problems 2, 3, 4, 5, and 6.

SMH 56, 57, 58

1.

$\dfrac{6}{6}$

2.

$\dfrac{8}{12}$

3.

$\dfrac{3}{4}$

4.

$\dfrac{12}{8}$

5.

$\dfrac{4}{3}$

6.

$\dfrac{5}{2}$

Ongoing Review

7. 130 − 73 = _____

A. 67   **B.** 63   **C.** 57   **D.** 53

Subtracting Fractions

Solve each problem and show your work. For the word problems, write an equation.

1. There was $\frac{7}{8}$ of a pan of brownies on the table. Some friends came over and ate $\frac{4}{8}$ of the pan of brownies. What fraction of the pan of brownies is left?

2. Marisol walks to school. The school is $\frac{6}{10}$ of a mile from her house. She has already walked $\frac{4}{10}$ of a mile. How much farther does Marisol have to walk?

3. There was $\frac{7}{12}$ of a gallon of milk in the refrigerator. The Jones family used $\frac{3}{12}$ of the gallon during breakfast. How much milk remains?

4. $\frac{4}{5} - \frac{2}{5} =$

5. $\frac{9}{12} - \frac{5}{12} =$

More Subtracting Fractions

NOTE Students solve subtraction problems involving fractions with like denominators.

Solve each problem and show your work. For the word problems, write an equation.

1. There is $\frac{7}{8}$ of a carton of juice in the refrigerator. The Ortega family drank $\frac{5}{8}$ of the carton with their breakfast. What fraction of the carton remains?

2. Venetta was walking to the library, which is $\frac{3}{4}$ of a mile away. She has walked $\frac{1}{4}$ of a mile. How much farther does Venetta have to walk?

3. Richard had $\frac{4}{5}$ of a bag of carrots. He fed $\frac{2}{5}$ of the bag to his rabbit. What fraction of the bag did Richard have left?

4. $\frac{7}{10} - \frac{4}{10} =$

5. $\frac{6}{8} - \frac{1}{8} =$

Fraction Cards and Decimal Squares

How to Make Fraction Cards

Materials for One Deck:

- 10 pieces of $8\frac{1}{2} \times 11$ inch colored oak tag or card stock, cut in fourths to make 40 cards
- *Student Activity Book* page 27, Fractions for Fraction Cards
- M16, Blank Wholes for Fraction Cards
- M17, Blank Thirds for Fraction Cards
- M18, Blank Fifths for Fraction Cards
- Scissors; glue sticks; rulers; colored pencils or crayons

Making the Cards:

1. Choose a fraction from the list of Fractions for Fraction Cards.

2. Write your fraction on a blank Fraction Card.

3. Use any of the "blanks" (blank wholes, blank thirds, or blank fifths) to make a picture for this fraction.

4. Cut out and glue your picture onto your Fraction Card above the name of the fraction. Your finished cards will look like this:

Fractions for Fraction Cards

$1\frac{3}{4}$	$\frac{1}{2}$	$1\frac{1}{2}$	$1\frac{1}{3}$
$\frac{4}{5}$	$1\frac{1}{4}$	$\frac{6}{8}$	$\frac{3}{6}$
$\frac{5}{3}$	$\frac{2}{4}$	$\frac{2}{6}$	$\frac{0}{4}$
$\frac{9}{4}$	$\frac{8}{6}$	$\frac{1}{4}$	$\frac{5}{4}$
$\frac{5}{6}$	$\frac{2}{5}$	$\frac{3}{12}$	$\frac{6}{3}$
$\frac{7}{8}$	$\frac{4}{10}$	$\frac{1}{5}$	$\frac{8}{12}$
$\frac{0}{2}$	$2\frac{1}{2}$	$\frac{8}{8}$	$\frac{3}{2}$
$\frac{2}{12}$	$\frac{1}{3}$	$\frac{9}{6}$	$\frac{2}{3}$
$\frac{1}{6}$	$\frac{3}{3}$	$\frac{4}{2}$	$\frac{1}{8}$
$\frac{5}{2}$	$\frac{3}{8}$	$\frac{3}{4}$	$\frac{4}{3}$

NOTE Students use addition and subtraction to solve problems about distances in miles.

SMH 13–15

How Many Miles?

The Kwan family is taking a trip across the United States. They started in New York, will drive to California, and then drive back. Solve the following problems about their mileage and explain how you found the difference between the numbers.

1. On July 1, they have gone 425 miles. How many more miles until they have gone 1,000 miles?

2. On July 5, they have gone 620 miles. How many more miles until they have gone 2,000 miles?

3. On July 20, they have gone 1,495 miles. How many more miles until they have gone 3,000 miles?

4. On August 1, they are about halfway back to New York. They have gone 4,690 miles. Their total trip will be about 6,000 miles. How many more miles do they still have to drive?

Ongoing Review

5. $5,010 -$ _____ $= 4,880$

   A. 30   **B.** 50   **C.** 130   **D.** 220

Combinations That Equal 1

Fill in the blanks to make each equation true. You may want to use the grids to help you model each problem.

NOTE Students find combinations of fractions with different denominators that equal 1. They use a 10 × 10 grid to model their work.

 59, 62

1. $\frac{1}{2} + \frac{1}{8} +$ _____ $= 1$

2. $\frac{2}{8} + \frac{1}{4} +$ _____ $= 1$

3. $\frac{1}{4} + \frac{3}{4} +$ _____ $= 1$

4. $\frac{2}{5} + \frac{5}{10} +$ _____ $= 1$

Fraction Subtraction

Solve each problem and show your work. For the word problems, write an equation.

NOTE Students solve subtraction problems involving fractions with like denominators.

1. There is $\frac{5}{6}$ of a pot of soup on the stove. The Kim family ate $\frac{4}{6}$ of the pot of soup. What fraction of the pot of soup remains?

2. Nadeem is walking to the park, which is $\frac{9}{10}$ of a mile away. He has walked $\frac{4}{10}$ of a mile. How much farther does Nadeem have to walk?

3. Tonya had $\frac{10}{12}$ of a yard of fabric. She used $\frac{5}{12}$ of a yard of fabric to make a lamp shade. What fraction of a yard of fabric is left?

4. $\frac{7}{8} - \frac{2}{8} =$

5. $\frac{3}{5} - \frac{1}{5} =$

What's the Fraction?

1. Here are pictures of some Fraction Cards. On each
one, write the name of the shaded fraction that is
shown.

Fraction: _____

Fraction: _____

Fraction: _____

Fraction: _____

2. Choose one of the fractions above and draw a picture
of an equivalent fraction.

3. How do you know these two fractions are equivalent?
Write in the space below or on another sheet of paper.

Is That True?

Decide if each equation is true or false.
Write T or F.

NOTE Students determine whether an equation involving fractions is true or false.

 59, 62

1. $\frac{1}{2} + \frac{1}{2} = 1$ _____

2. $\frac{1}{4} + \frac{1}{4} = \frac{1}{2}$ _____

3. $\frac{2}{4} = \frac{1}{2}$ _____

4. $\frac{1}{8} + \frac{1}{8} = \frac{1}{16}$ _____

5. $\frac{1}{4} + \frac{1}{4} + \frac{1}{4} + \frac{1}{4} = 1$ _____

6. $\frac{1}{2} + \frac{1}{4} + \frac{1}{8} + \frac{1}{16} = 1$ _____

7. $\frac{1}{16} + \frac{1}{16} = \frac{1}{8}$ _____

8. $\frac{1}{4} + \frac{1}{8} + \frac{1}{8} = \frac{1}{2}$ _____

9. $\frac{4}{8} = \frac{1}{4}$ _____

10. $\frac{2}{4} = \frac{4}{8}$ _____

Ongoing Review

11. If you take an elevator from the second floor below ground level to the 18th floor, how many floors have you traveled?

   A. 36   **B.** 22   **C.** 20   **D.** 16

Finding Equivalent Fractions

As you are playing *Capture Fractions,* keep track of the matches you make by writing equations that show equivalent fractions.

Example: $\frac{1}{2} = \frac{4}{8}$

I found these equivalent fractions:

Reading a Long Book

Solve these problems. Show your work.

NOTE Students practice solving addition and subtraction problems in a story problem context.

SMH 8–9, 13–15

1. Ravi is reading a book that is 1,200 pages long. So far, he has read 189 pages. How many more pages does he have to read to finish the book?

2. Over the next three weeks, Ravi reads 342 more pages. How many pages has he read so far?

3. At the end of six weeks, Ravi has read 977 pages. How many more pages does he have left to finish the book?

Ongoing Review

4. How many tens are there in 3,102?

   A. 31   **B.** 310   **C.** 3,100   **D.** 3,102

© Pearson Education 4

Which Is Larger?

Which is larger, $\frac{2}{3}$ or $\frac{3}{2}$? Use words and pictures to explain your answer.

NOTE Students compare pairs of fractions.

SMH 60–61

Fractions in Containers

More than one whole

One whole

Between one half and one whole

One half

$\frac{3}{6}$

Less than one half

Write each fraction in the container in which it belongs.

Cross out each fraction as you use it. ($\frac{3}{6}$ has been done for you.)

There are five fractions for each container.

$\frac{3}{6}$ $\frac{5}{5}$ $\frac{1}{4}$ $\frac{5}{2}$ $\frac{1}{5}$ $\frac{2}{3}$ $\frac{3}{5}$ $\frac{5}{7}$ $\frac{6}{3}$ $\frac{2}{5}$ $\frac{3}{3}$

$\frac{10}{20}$ $\frac{3}{10}$ $\frac{10}{5}$ $\frac{2}{6}$ $\frac{3}{2}$ $\frac{9}{10}$ $\frac{10}{10}$ $\frac{4}{8}$ $\frac{4}{5}$ $\frac{8}{8}$ $\frac{2}{4}$

$\frac{6}{5}$ $\frac{2}{2}$ $\frac{6}{12}$

Comparing Fractions

NOTE Students decide which of two fractions is greater and put the fractions in order on a number line.

SMH **60–61**

1. Circle the larger fraction in each pair.

   Write = if you think that the fractions are equal.

   Next to each pair, show or write how you decided.

   a. $\frac{5}{8}$ $\frac{1}{2}$

   b. $\frac{3}{4}$ $\frac{7}{8}$

   c. $\frac{2}{3}$ $\frac{3}{2}$

2. Put these fractions in order from smallest to largest.
   Use the clothesline below to order them.

   $\frac{1}{2}$ $\frac{3}{8}$ $\frac{9}{5}$ $\frac{1}{6}$ $\frac{3}{2}$

© Pearson Education 4

Making Fraction Number Lines

With half of your group's deck of Fraction Cards, make a number line by laying each card out in order from least to greatest. Use your Landmark Cards (0, $\frac{1}{2}$, 1, and 2) to help you. Record where you place each fraction on the number lines below.

School Supplies

NOTE Students practice solving addition and subtraction problems in a story problem context involving money.

SMH 8–9, 13–15

1. Leah had $15.00 to spend on school supplies. She spent $3.75 on pencils, $2.55 on a pencil sharpener, and $5.25 on paper.

   a. How much money did she spend on supplies?

   b. After buying the supplies, how much of her $15.00 is left?

2. Diego purchases a dictionary for $12.89 and notebooks for $5.49.

   a. How much money did he spend on these supplies?

   b. If he pays $20.00, how much change will he receive?

Ongoing Review

3. Which fraction is equal to $\frac{1}{8}$?

   A. $\frac{2}{18}$ **B.** $\frac{2}{4}$ **C.** $\frac{8}{16}$ **D.** $\frac{2}{16}$

More or Less Than 1?

Fill in $<$, $>$, or $=$ to make each equation true.

NOTE Students find combinations of fractions that equal 1 and decide which of two fractions is greater. Students can use the 10 $\times$ 10 squares to help them think through their ideas about fractional parts of wholes.

SMH 60–62

1. $\frac{1}{4} + \frac{2}{4}$ _____ 1

2. 1 _____ $\frac{1}{2} + \frac{1}{4} + \frac{1}{8} + \frac{1}{16}$

3. $\frac{2}{3} + \frac{2}{3}$ _____ 1

4. $\frac{3}{4}$ _____ $\frac{4}{5}$

5. $\frac{1}{2} + \frac{5}{5}$ _____ 1

Write fractions in the blanks to make each equation true.

6. _____ + _____ > 1

7. _____ + _____ < 1

8. _____ + _____ $= 1$

42　Unit 6

Name _____   Date _____

Fraction Cards and Decimal Squares   **Daily Practice**

Make Your Move

The fractions on each clothesline are out of order.
Show how to fix the order with just one move.

NOTE Students put fractions in the correct order.

SMH 60–61

1.

I need to move the $\frac{3}{8}$. $\frac{1}{4}$ is the same as $\frac{2}{8}$, and $\frac{1}{2}$ is the same as $\frac{4}{8}$. So $\frac{3}{8}$ should go between them.

2.

3.

4.

5.

Ongoing Review

6. Which total is **less than** 100?

A. 44 + 54   **B.** 53 + 57   **C.** 81 + 20   **D.** 76 + 24

© Pearson Education 4

Session 2.6   Unit 6   **43**

Butterfly Wingspans (page 1 of 2)

Yuki went to the Natural History Museum to study butterflies. The information he has about some of the butterflies in the collection is shown below.

Name	Wingspan (inches)	Name	Wingspan (inches)
American Snout	$1\frac{1}{2}$	Pearl Crescent	$1\frac{5}{8}$
Giant Swallowtail	$5\frac{1}{4}$	Postman	$2\frac{1}{2}$
Julia	$3\frac{1}{2}$	Red Admiral	$3\frac{1}{8}$
Milbert's Tortoiseshell	$2\frac{5}{8}$	Saturn	$4\frac{1}{4}$
Monarch	$3\frac{1}{2}$	Tiger Swallowtail	$3\frac{3}{4}$
Painted Lady	$2\frac{1}{2}$	Viceroy	$2\frac{7}{8}$

Record the measurements on the line plot below.

Butterfly Wingspans (inches)

Write three statements that describe the data.

Butterfly Wingspans (page 2 of 2)

Use the information on the previous page to solve
the following problems. Show your work.

1. How much longer is the wingspan of the Viceroy butterfly than
the wingspan of the Pearl Crescent butterfly?

2. How much longer is the wingspan of the Giant Swallowtail
butterfly than the wingspan of the Tiger Swallowtail butterfly?

3. The American Snout butterfly and the Postman butterfly are
side-by-side. What is the length of their combined wingspans?

4. How much longer is the wingspan of the Red Admiral butterfly
than the wingspan of Milbert's Tortoiseshell butterfly?

5. The Pearl Crescent butterfly and the Viceroy butterfly are side-
by-side. What is the length of their combined wingspans?

6. The Saturn butterfly and the Tiger Swallowtail butterfly are side-
by-side. What is the length of their combined wingspans?

Pepper's Puppies

Cheyenne's dog, Pepper, had puppies. Cheyenne recorded their weights in the line plot below.

> **NOTE** Students solve addition and subtraction problems involving fractions using data given in a line plot.

Weights of Pepper's Puppies (pounds)

Solve each problem and show your work.

1. Two puppies weighed the same amount. What was the total weight of the two puppies?

2. How many more pounds did the heaviest puppy weigh than the lightest puppy?

3. The heaviest puppy gained $\frac{4}{8}$ of a pound in its first month. How much did it weigh after the first month?

Multiplying Whole Numbers and Fractions

Use a representation to solve each problem. For each word problem, write a multiplication equation that represents the problem.

1. Jake bought three kinds of pizza for a party. Each pizza was the same size. People were not very hungry, and at the end of the party there was $\frac{3}{4}$ of each pizza left. How much pizza was left in all?

2. A class is counting by $\frac{2}{6}$s. What number does the 7th person say?

3. $6 \times \frac{1}{3} =$

4. $3 \times \frac{3}{8} =$

Chunks of Cheese

NOTE Students solve problems involving multiplication of a whole number and a fraction.

Morris Mouse's Cheese House sells chunks of cheese. Each chunk weighs $\frac{3}{4}$ of a pound. Find the total weight of each kind of cheese. Use a representation to solve each problem. Also, write a multiplication equation that represents the problem. Show your work.

1. 5 chunks of cheddar cheese

Total weight _____

2. 10 chunks of Swiss cheese

Total weight _____

3. 4 chunks of American cheese

Total weight _____

4. 8 chunks of parmesan cheese

Total weight _____

Multiplying Fractions and Whole Numbers

Use a representation to solve each problem. For each word problem, write a multiplication equation that represents the problem.

1. A grocery store sells bags of 9 apples. Anna used $\frac{2}{3}$ of the apples in a bag in an apple pie. How many apples did she use in the pie?

2. Steve was in a 7 mile race. He ran $\frac{1}{2}$ of it and walked the rest. How many miles did he run?

3. $\frac{2}{3} \times 12 =$

4. There are 10 boys in class. $\frac{4}{5}$ of them have brown hair. How many boys have brown hair?

5. $\frac{5}{8} \times 16 =$

6. $\frac{1}{2} \times 11 =$

More Multiplying Fractions and Whole Numbers

Use a representation to solve each problem. For each word problem, write a multiplication equation that represents the problem.

1. Sabrina walks to school. Her house is $\frac{3}{8}$ of a mile from school. How many miles would she walk to and from school in 5 days?

2. $6 \times \frac{2}{5} =$

3. Damian has a recipe that calls for $\frac{2}{3}$ of a cup of flour. He wants to make 4 times the recipe. How much flour does he need?

4. $3 \times \frac{3}{4} =$

Multiplying with Fractions

NOTE Students solve problems involving multiplication of whole numbers and fractions.

Use a representation to solve each problem. For each word problem, write a multiplication equation that represents the problem.

1. $4 \times \frac{1}{5} =$

2. $\frac{3}{4} \times 16 =$

3. $\frac{1}{6} \times 9 =$

4. $12 \times \frac{1}{2} =$

5. Mr. Garcia has 15 grandchildren. $\frac{2}{3}$ of them are girls. How many are girls?

6. Helena needs 8 pieces of wire. Each piece needs to be $\frac{3}{4}$ of a foot long. What is the total length of the wire Helena needs?

Multiplying Fractions

Use a representation to solve each problem. For
each word problem, write a multiplication equation
that represents the problem.

1. In the store Damian found pretzels that came in $\frac{1}{3}$-pound bags.
He bought 5 bags of pretzels. How many pounds of pretzels
did he buy?

2. $3 \times \frac{6}{8} =$

3. There were 25 students in class. One day, $\frac{3}{5}$ of them wore
sneakers. How many students wore sneakers?

4. $\frac{7}{10} \times 4 =$

5. Jill used stones that were each $\frac{3}{4}$ of a foot high to build a wall.
She piled 6 stones on top of each other. How many feet high
was her wall?

6. $\frac{5}{6} \times 12 =$

All Kinds of Nuts

Use a representation to solve each problem. Also, write an equation that represents the problem.

> **NOTE** Students solve problems involving multiplication of whole numbers and fractions.

1. Emaan bought 6 bags of walnuts. Each bag contained $\frac{3}{4}$ of a pound of walnuts. What was the total weight of the walnuts?

2. A man bought 12 boxes of nuts. He took $\frac{1}{6}$ of the boxes to his office. How many boxes of nuts did he take to the office?

3. Kimberly is making 3 loaves of nut bread. For each loaf, she needs $\frac{3}{4}$ of a cup of pecans. How many cups of pecans does she need? Circle the best answer below.

between 3 and 4 cups

between 2 and 3 cups

between 1 and 2 cups

Decimal Grids (page 1 of 2)

Whole

Grid A

Fraction Cards and Decimal Squares

Decimal Grids (page 2 of 2)

Grid B

Grid C

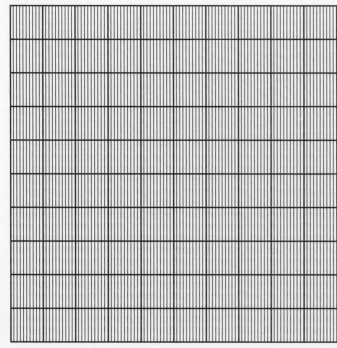

Stamp Collection

NOTE Students practice solving addition and subtraction problems in a story problem context.

SMH 8–9, 13–15

1. José has a collection of stamps. He has 399 stamps from North America and 218 stamps from South America.

   a. How many stamps does José have?

   b. How many more stamps does he need to have 800 altogether?

2. Aliyah also has a stamp collection. She has 441 North American stamps and 183 European stamps.

   a. How many stamps does Aliyah have?

   b. How many more stamps does she need to have 800 altogether?

3. Who has more stamps, José or Aliyah? By how many stamps?

© Pearson Education 4

Everyday Uses of Fractions and Decimals

Look for everyday uses of fractions and decimals. List what you find below. Try looking in the newspaper, in your cupboards, and all around your home.

NOTE Students learn about decimals and how they relate to fractions. At home, they will look for examples of how fractions and decimals are used in the real world.

SMH 53, 64

Everyday uses of fractions:

Everyday uses of decimals:

Bug Collections

The science class collected crickets and beetles. The students made line plots to show the lengths of the insects.

> **NOTE** Students solve addition and subtraction problems involving fractions using data given in a line plot.

Lengths of Crickets (inches)

Lengths of Beetles (inches)

1. How much longer is the longest cricket than the shortest cricket?

_____

2. How much longer is the longest beetle than the shortest beetle?

_____

3. The cricket Benson found is $1\frac{1}{8}$ inches long. How much longer is this cricket than the shortest one in the collection?

_____

4. The beetle Tonya found is $1\frac{1}{4}$ inches long. How much shorter is this beetle than the longest one in the collection?

_____

Fraction Cards and Decimal Squares

Selling Fruit

NOTE Students practice solving addition and subtraction problems in a story problem context.

SMH 8–9, 13–15

1. On Monday, a grocery store received a shipment of 700 peaches. The store sold 567 of them that day. How many peaches were left to sell the next day?

2. On Wednesday, the store received a shipment of 850 grapefruits. The store sold 362 grapefruits that day. How many grapefruits were left to sell the next day?

3. On Saturday, the store received a shipment of 1,500 melons. The store sold 734 melons on Saturday and 674 melons on Sunday.

   a. How many melons did they sell on the weekend (Saturday and Sunday)?

   b. How many melons were left to sell on Monday morning?

Ongoing Review

4. Which number is "three tenths"?

   A. 0.03   **B.** 0.3   **C.** 3.0   **D.** 3.10

Showing Decimals on a 10 × 10 Square

Show the following decimal numbers on the squares below by shading in each amount. Each square represents 1.

> **NOTE** Students shade in decimal numbers on a square that represents 1.
>
> **SMH** 65–68

0.7

1.

0.75

2.

0.5

3.

0.38

4.

More Showing Decimals on a 10 × 10 Square

NOTE Students represent decimals on a square that represents 1.

 SMH 65

Show the following decimal numbers on the squares below by shading in each amount. Each square represents 1.

0.1

1.

0.45

2.

0.6

3.

0.95

4.

Runner's Log (page 1 of 2)

Tony made a log of how many miles he ran during
a week.

Day	Mileage	Comments
Monday	2.2 miles	I ran around the pond once.
Tuesday	1.5 miles	I ran on the track, six times around.
Wednesday	1.25 miles	I ran on the track again.
Thursday	0 miles	I was tired and took the day off.
Friday	2.9 miles	I was visiting my aunt and ran with her.
Saturday	0.8 mile	I was worn out from yesterday.
Sunday	1 mile	I ran pretty slowly.

1. How far did Tony run this week? _____

2. Show how you figured it out.

Runner's Log (page 2 of 2)

Dana: $9\frac{1}{2}$ years old; has run two races before

Day	Mileage	Comments
Monday	1.75 miles	I ran with my mom to the store, but we got a ride back.
Tuesday	1.6 miles	Jamie and I ran to school because we were late!
Wednesday	0 miles	I had to babysit today, so I could not run.
Thursday	3.2 miles	I ran slowly, but much farther than before.
Friday	0.5 miles	I was really tired, so I only ran around the track twice.
Saturday	1.75 miles	I ran home from the store, but slowly.
Sunday	0.8 mile	I ran pretty fast, but not very far.

3. How many miles did Dana run? _____

4. Show how you figured it out.

Coin Jars

NOTE Students solve problems about combinations of coins.

 SMH 70–71

1. Quincy has a coin jar full of pennies, dimes, nickels, and quarters. He knows that there is $4.50 in his coin jar. What combination of coins could be in Quincy's coin jar that would equal $4.50?

First solution: Second solution:

2. Petra also has a coin jar. There are only two kinds of coins in her coin jar. She knows that there is $3.90 in her jar. What combination of coins could be in Petra's coin jar that would equal $3.90?

First solution: Second solution:

Ongoing Review

3. Which number is less than 0.5?

A. 0.05   **B.** 0.55   **C.** .5   **D.** 0.50

Which Is More?

Circle the decimal that is a larger amount. Explain how you figured out which is more.

NOTE Students work with and compare some common decimals in order to decide which number is larger.

SMH 69

1.　　0.5　　　or　　　0.45

2.　　0.10　　or　　　0.01

3.　　0.5　　　or　　　0.50

Buying Fabric

Use a representation to solve each problem.
For each word problem, write a multiplication
equation that represents the problem.

NOTE Students solve problems involving
multiplication of a whole number by a
fraction.

1. Bill bought 6 pieces of yellow fabric. Each piece was $\frac{1}{3}$ of a
   yard long. How many yards of fabric did Bill buy in all?

2. Kimberly bought 2 pieces of blue fabric. Each piece was $\frac{7}{8}$ of a
   yard long. How many yards of fabric did Kimberly buy in all?

3. Alejandro bought 7 pieces of red fabric. Each piece was $\frac{3}{4}$ of a
   yard long. How many yards of fabric did Alejandro buy in all?

4. $2 \times \frac{3}{10} =$

5. $9 \times \frac{1}{6} =$

Make a Running Log (page 1 of 2)

Make an imaginary running log. Fill in the mileage for each day. Make sure that your total mileage for the week is 10.5.

Log 1: Each distance must include tenths or hundredths.

Day	Mileage	Comments

How did you make the miles add up to 10.5?
How did you think about this problem?

Make a Running Log (page 2 of 2)

Make an imaginary running log. Fill in the mileage for each day. Make sure that your total mileage for the week is 10.5.

Log 2: Day 1 is 2.3 miles and Day 5 is 1.7 miles.

Fill in the rest to make a total of 10.5 miles.

Day	Mileage	Comments
1	2.3 miles	
5	1.7 miles	

How did you make the miles add up to 10.5?
How did you think about this problem?

Comparing Fractions 2

Circle the greater fraction.

> **NOTE** Students determine which is the greater fraction in each pair.
>
> **SMH** 60–61

1. $\frac{1}{3}$ $\frac{3}{5}$ 2. $\frac{5}{6}$ $\frac{2}{3}$

3. $\frac{1}{2}$ $\frac{1}{8}$ 4. $\frac{3}{10}$ $\frac{3}{5}$

5. $\frac{4}{5}$ $\frac{1}{2}$ 6. $\frac{7}{10}$ $\frac{1}{4}$

7. $\frac{3}{8}$ $\frac{5}{8}$ 8. $\frac{2}{3}$ $\frac{3}{4}$

9. $\frac{1}{4}$ $\frac{3}{8}$ 10. $\frac{4}{8}$ $\frac{3}{5}$

11. $\frac{9}{10}$ $\frac{4}{5}$ 12. $\frac{2}{8}$ $\frac{1}{3}$

Ongoing Review

13. Which shows the fractions in order from least to greatest?

     A. $\frac{1}{2}, \frac{3}{8}, \frac{1}{6}$ **C.** $\frac{3}{8}, \frac{1}{2}, \frac{1}{6}$

     B. $\frac{1}{6}, \frac{3}{8}, \frac{1}{2}$ **D.** $\frac{1}{6}, \frac{1}{2}, \frac{3}{8}$

Multiplying with Fractions

NOTE Students solve problems involving multiplication of whole numbers and fractions.

Use a representation to solve each problem. For each word problem, write a multiplication equation that represents the problem.

1. $\frac{1}{5} \times 8 =$

2. $6 \times \frac{2}{3} =$

3. $2 \times \frac{5}{6} =$

4. $\frac{7}{8} \times 8 =$

5. LaTanya had a piece of fabric that was 3 yards long. She used $\frac{1}{2}$ of it to make a skirt. How much of the fabric did she use?

6. Benson had 16 marbles. He gave $\frac{3}{8}$ of them away. How many marbles did he give away?

Working Hard

Use a representation to solve each problem. Also, write an equation that represents the problem.

NOTE Students solve problems involving multiplication of whole numbers and fractions.

1. Last week, Ms. Cortez sold 24 computers. $\frac{5}{8}$ of them were laptops. How many laptops did Ms. Cortez sell?

2. An office building has 14 offices, all the same size. A painter uses $\frac{3}{4}$ of a gallon of paint to paint one office ceiling. How much paint will the painter need to paint all of the office ceilings?

3. Mr. Stein bikes to work. The roundtrip distance he bikes each day is $\frac{7}{8}$ of a mile. What is the total distance he bikes in 5 days? Circle the best answer below.

between 6 and 7 miles

between 5 and 6 miles

between 4 and 5 miles

How Many Hundreds?
How Many Altogether?

NOTE Students estimate and solve addition problems.

SMH 8–9

Number of Postcards in Six Collections	About how many hundreds altogether? Estimate.	Add the numbers to find the exact total.

61   14   52
  39   59
    98
	100 or 200 or 300 or 400?
	How did you decide?	

Cost of Four Items at the Grocery Store	About how many dollars altogether? Estimate.	Add the numbers to find the exact total.
$0.91 $2.41 $1.77 $3.04	$6.00 or $7.00 or $8.00 or $9.00 How did you decide?	

Summer Sale!

Belinda's Toys and Hobby Shop is having a
summer sale. Here are some of the sale items.

NOTE Students calculate
and compare fractional
parts of groups.

SMH 55

$6.00 $20.00   PUZZLE GAME $12.00 $15.00

1. Calculate the sale prices.

   $\frac{1}{4}$ off a stuffed animal _____ $\frac{1}{3}$ off a book _____
   You saved $_____   You saved $_____

   $\frac{1}{2}$ off a puzzle _____ $\frac{1}{5}$ off a board game _____
   You saved $_____   You saved $_____

2. Which discount is greater?

   a. $\frac{1}{3}$ off 2 stuffed animals or $\frac{1}{4}$ off 4 books _____
   Explain your thinking.

   b. $\frac{1}{3}$ off a puzzle or $\frac{1}{3}$ off 3 books _____
   Explain your thinking.

Polished Spiral Karin Kuhlmann

"Although the creation of fractals is bounded to strict mathematical rules, the results are always very inspiring." – **Karin Kuhlmann**

Investigations
IN NUMBER, DATA, AND SPACE®

Moving Between Solids and Silhouettes

Geometric Solids

cube

rectangular prism

octagonal prism

cylinder

hemisphere

cone

hexagonal prism

square pyramid

triangular prism

sphere

cylinder

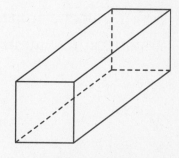

square prism

Comparing Decimals

Fill in <, >, or = to make each expression true.

NOTE Students compare the sizes of different decimals.

 69

1. 0.15 _____ 1.5

2. 0.05 _____ 0.5

3. 0.3 _____ 0.25

4. 0.95 _____ 0.9

5. 0.60 _____ 0.6

6. 0.85 _____ 0.05

7. 0.55 _____ 0.01

8. 0.95 _____ 1.0

Sharing 60

Solve these problems and explain your solutions.

NOTE Students find fractions of a group of objects.

SMH 62

There are 60 milk cartons in a crate.

1. Mr. Daniel's class took $\frac{1}{2}$ of the milk cartons in the crate. How many milk cartons did they take?

2. Ms. Kim's class took $\frac{1}{6}$ of the milk cartons in the crate. How many milk cartons did they take?

3. Ms. Glasgow's class took $\frac{1}{5}$ of the milk cartons in the crate. How many milk cartons did they take?

4. Show each fraction on the 5 × 12 grid below. Label each piece.

Silhouettes of Geometric Solids

A

B

C

D

E

F

H

G

K

I

J

L

M

N

Moving Between Solids and Silhouettes

Don't Block My Shadow

Circle all the silhouettes that can be made with each solid.

NOTE Students determine which silhouettes can be made from a given solid.

SMH 122–123

1.

2.

3.

Ongoing Review

4. Which shape has only flat surfaces?

A. 　　B. 　　C. 　　D.

Landscape 1

Build this landscape with your geometric solids. Then look at each pair of silhouettes below. Find all of the points in the landscape from which you could see both silhouettes in a pair. Write the letters of these points beside the silhouettes.

Pair 1
Points from which these could be seen:

_____

Pair 2
Points from which these could be seen:

_____

Pair 3
Points from which these could be seen:

_____

Fill-In Fractions

Fill in the box for each fraction so that it
represents the amount stated for each box.
The first fraction has been done for you.

NOTE Students place fractions
equal to or between landmarks.

 60–61

---

1. Less than $\frac{1}{2}$

$$\frac{3}{8} \qquad \frac{3}{\boxed{}} \qquad \frac{\boxed{}}{5}$$

2. $\frac{1}{2}$

$$\frac{\boxed{}}{4} \qquad \frac{5}{\boxed{}} \qquad \frac{\boxed{}}{12}$$

---

3. Between $\frac{1}{2}$ and 1

$$\frac{2}{\boxed{}} \qquad \frac{\boxed{}}{6} \qquad \frac{3}{\boxed{}}$$

4. 1

$$\frac{\boxed{}}{3} \qquad \frac{\boxed{}}{8} \qquad \frac{2}{\boxed{}}$$

---

5. Between 1 and $1\frac{1}{2}$

$$\frac{\boxed{}}{8} \qquad \frac{6}{\boxed{}} \qquad \frac{5}{\boxed{}}$$

6. More than $1\frac{1}{2}$

$$\frac{5}{\boxed{}} \qquad \frac{\boxed{}}{3} \qquad \frac{4}{\boxed{}}$$

Mystery Silhouettes

List objects you find at home that make silhouettes that are these shapes. The size of the silhouette does not have to match.

NOTE Students have been studying the silhouettes (shadows) of geometric shapes. Using a flashlight or other bright light will help students find silhouettes.

SMH 122–123

1.   Object(s) I found that make a square silhouette:

_____

_____

2.   Object(s) I found that make a triangular silhouette:

_____

_____

3.   Object(s) I found that make both a rectangular silhouette and a circular silhouette:

_____

_____

Landscape 2

Build this landscape with your geometric solids. Then look at each pair of silhouettes below. Find all of the points in the landscape from which you could see both silhouettes in a pair. Write the letters of these points beside the silhouettes.

Pair 1

Points from which these could be seen:

_____

Pair 2

Points from which these could be seen:

_____

Pair 3

Points from which these could be seen:

_____

Landscape 3

Build this landscape with your geometric solids. Then look at each pair of silhouettes below. Find all of the points in the landscape from which you could see both silhouettes in a pair. Write the letters of these points beside the silhouettes.

Pair 1

Points from which these could be seen:

_____

Pair 2

Points from which these could be seen:

_____

Pair 3

Points from which these could be seen:

_____

Landscape Challenge

Look at this pair of silhouettes. Find all of the points in the three geometric landscapes from which these two silhouettes could be seen. Write the letters of these points from *Student Activity Book* pages 7, 11, and 12.

These could be seen from the following points:

In Landscape 1:

_____

_____

_____

_____

In Landscape 2:

_____

_____

_____

_____

In Landscape 3:

_____

_____

_____

_____

How Many Waffles?

Solve each problem. Use pictures and words to show how you solved each problem.

NOTE Students find the total amount given the number of fractional parts.

 58, 62

1. Three people each get $1\frac{3}{4}$ waffles. How many waffles are there in all? Draw a picture and tell how many.

_____ waffles in all

2. Draw a picture to show how four people could each have $2\frac{1}{3}$ waffles. Tell how many waffles in all.

_____ waffles in all

© Pearson Education 4

Fractions: Which Is Bigger?

Circle the larger fraction. Explain
how you knew which fraction is larger.

NOTE Students compare the
value of different fractions.

SMH 60–61

1. $\dfrac{3}{4}$ $\dfrac{3}{2}$

2. $1\dfrac{1}{5}$ $\dfrac{3}{2}$

3. $\dfrac{2}{4}$ $\dfrac{4}{8}$

4. $\dfrac{5}{6}$ $\dfrac{6}{5}$

Make the Buildings (page 1 of 2)

1.

2.

3.

4.

5.

Make the Buildings (page 2 of 2)

6.

7.

8.

9.

10.

Books to Read

NOTE Students find fractions of a group of objects.

SMH 55

Solve these problems and explain your solutions.

There are 48 books on the reading list.

1. Luke read $\frac{1}{3}$ of the books on the reading list. How many books did he read?

2. Yuson read $\frac{3}{8}$ of the books on the reading list. How many books did she read?

3. Alejandro read $\frac{4}{6}$ of the books on the reading list. How many books did he read?

4. a. Who read the most books on the reading list?

b. What fraction of the reading list does he or she have left to read?

How Many Cubes?

How many cubes does it take to make each building?

NOTE Student have been making cube buildings and finding the volume of these buildings.

1.

_____ cubes

2.

_____ cubes

3.

_____ cubes

Moving Between Solids and Silhouettes

Drawing Silhouettes: An Introduction

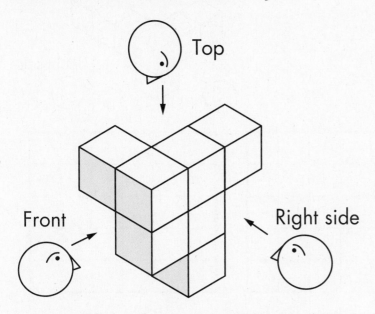

Top

Front   Right side

Use cubes to make this building.

Two silhouettes of the building are shown below.

One was seen from the front, and one was seen from the right side.

The silhouettes are drawn on graph paper so that we can see where the cubes are.

What do you think the top silhouette looks like?

Front   Top   Right side

Front, Top, and Side Silhouettes (page 1 of 2)

Make each building with cubes.

Then draw the silhouettes for both.

Building 1:

Front

Top, as seen from the front

Right side

Building 2:

Front

Top, as seen from the front

Right side

Front, Top, and Side Silhouettes (page 2 of 2)

Make each building with cubes.

Then draw the silhouettes for both.

Building 3:

Front   Top, as seen from the front   Right side

Building 4:

Front   Top, as seen from the front   Right side

Is That True?

NOTE Students practice adding fractions.

SMH 62

Determine whether each equation is true or false.
Write T or F after each equation.

1. $\frac{2}{5} + \frac{1}{10} = \frac{1}{2}$ _____

2. $\frac{5}{6} = \frac{2}{3}$ _____

3. $\frac{1}{4} + \frac{1}{4} = \frac{1}{8}$ _____

4. $\frac{1}{8} + \frac{1}{8} = \frac{1}{4}$ _____

5. $\frac{1}{2} + \frac{1}{3} = \frac{4}{6}$ _____

Fill in the blank(s) to make these equations true.

6. _____ + _____ = 1

7. $\frac{1}{2}$ + _____ = $\frac{3}{4}$

8. $\frac{3}{5}$ + _____ = $1\frac{1}{5}$

Decimals: Which Is Bigger?

NOTE Students compare the size of different decimals.

SMH 69

Circle the larger decimal. Explain how you figured out each one.

1.   0.05   0.5

2.   0.33   0.2

3.   0.75   0.7

4.   1.2   2.1

Drawing Silhouettes A and B

A. Draw the three silhouettes
for this building. Do not use cubes.

Front   Top, as seen from the front   Right side

B. Make the building with cubes.
Then draw the three silhouettes.

Front   Top, as seen from the front   Right side

Drawing Silhouettes C and D

C. Draw the three silhouettes
for this building. Do not use cubes.

Front

Top, as seen from the front

Right side

D. Make the building with cubes.
Then draw the three silhouettes.

Front

Top, as seen from the front

Right side

Castle Builder

A student built a "castle" from blocks. Label the silhouettes below *front*, *back*, *left*, and *right*.

1.

_____

2.

_____

3.

_____

4.

_____

Left — Back — Right — Front

Ongoing Review

5. Choose the silhouette that is the correct one for the top of this cube building.

Top

TOP

TOP

TOP

Building from Silhouettes

For each puzzle below, construct a cube building that makes the three silhouettes. Do any other buildings also make these silhouettes?

1.

Front

Top, as seen from the front

Right side

2.

Front

Top, as seen from the front

Right side

3.

Front

Top, as seen from the front

Right side

Challenge: How many different cube buildings make three silhouettes in Puzzle 1? In Puzzle 2? In Puzzle 3?

Daily Practice

Decimal Problems

Solve each problem by using Steve's running log below. Use another sheet of paper to solve the problems.

> **NOTE** Students compare and add decimals using a running log.
>
> **SMH** 70–71

Day	Mileage	Comments
Monday	2.2 miles	I ran around the pond once.
Tuesday	1.50 miles	I ran on the track six times around.
Wednesday	1.25 miles	I ran on the track again.
Thursday	0 miles	I was tired and took a day off.
Friday	2.9 miles	I was visiting my aunt and ran with her.
Saturday	0.8 mile	I was worn out from yesterday.
Sunday	1 mile	I ran pretty slowly.

1. a. On what 4 days did Steve run the farthest?

b. How many miles did he run during those 4 days?

2. a. On what 3 days did Steve run the shortest distance?

b. How many miles did he run during those 3 days?

Showing Decimals on a Grid

Show the following decimals on the grids below.
Label each grid.

NOTE Students represent decimals on 10 × 10 grids.

SMH 65, 66, 67, 68

0.1   0.95   0.08   0.76

Different Views of a City

This map shows the top view of a cube city.

The eight buildings shown are made from connecting cubes.

The number on each building tells how many cubes high that building is.

A photographer flew around the city in a helicopter and took four silhouette photographs.

The photographs were taken from points A, B, C, and D (looking in the directions of the arrows).

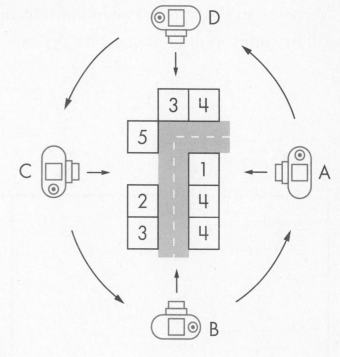

The resulting silhouettes are shown here. Below each one, write the letter of the point where it was taken.

1. _____   **2.** _____   **3.** _____   **4.** _____

Equivalent Fractions

Write each fraction below in the appropriate box.
All fractions in the box must be equal.

$\dfrac{2}{12}$ $\dfrac{2}{8}$ $\dfrac{2}{4}$ $\dfrac{4}{12}$ $\dfrac{3}{6}$ $\dfrac{3}{12}$

$\dfrac{5}{10}$ $\dfrac{9}{12}$ $\dfrac{4}{6}$ $\dfrac{2}{6}$ $\dfrac{8}{12}$ $\dfrac{6}{8}$

$\dfrac{1}{2}$	$\dfrac{1}{3}$
$\dfrac{1}{4}$	$\dfrac{2}{3}$
$\dfrac{3}{4}$	$\dfrac{1}{6}$

How Many Cubes?

How many cubes fit in each box? First, determine the answer without building the box. Then build a box and use cubes to check. Compare your first answer to the actual answer before going on to the next box.

Think about a way you could determine the number of cubes that would fit in any box.

	Pattern	**Picture**	**First Answer**	**Actual Answer**
Box 1			_____	_____
Box 2			_____	_____
Box 3			_____	_____

Fraction Story Problems

Solve each problem and show your solution.

NOTE Students solve fraction problems in a story context.

SMH 53–55, 62

1. There was a quart of milk in the refrigerator. Venetta drank $\frac{1}{4}$ of the quart. Steve drank $\frac{1}{8}$ of the quart. Kimberly drank $\frac{2}{8}$ of the quart.

    a. How much milk did Venetta, Steve, and Kimberly drink in all?

    b. How much milk is left?

2. There were 30 crackers on a plate. Lucy ate $\frac{1}{6}$ of the crackers, Abdul ate $\frac{1}{5}$ of the crackers, and Emaan ate $\frac{1}{3}$ of the crackers.

    a. Who ate the most crackers? How many crackers did he or she eat?

    b. How many crackers are left?

Comparing Decimals

Fill in <, >, or = to make each expression true.

1. 0.25 _____ 0.3

2. 0.71 _____ 0.09

3. 0.33 _____ 0.30

4. 0.02 _____ 0.17

5. 0.46 _____ 0.54

Write decimals in the blanks to make each equation true.

6. _____ + _____ > 1

7. _____ + _____ < 1

8. _____ + _____ = 1

Making Boxes from the Bottom Up (page 1 of 4)

The dark squares make the bottom of a rectangular box that contains exactly 20 cubes. The box has no top. Draw the sides to finish the pattern for the box.

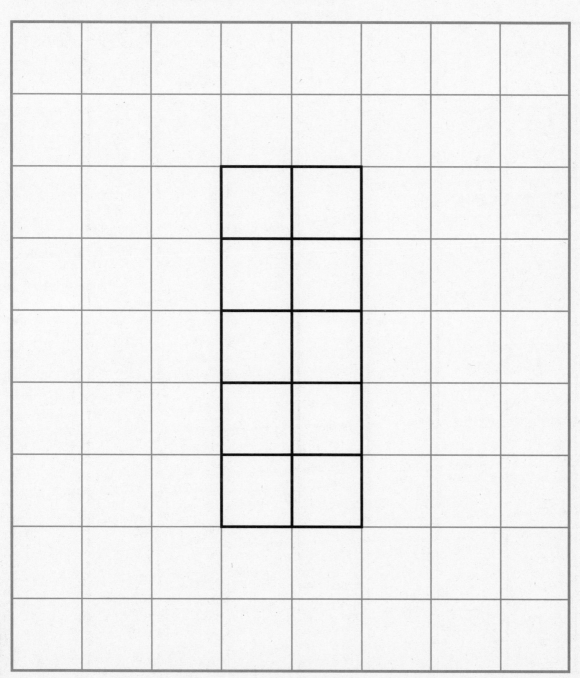

Making Boxes from the Bottom Up (page 2 of 4)

The dark squares make the bottom of a rectangular box that contains exactly 12 cubes. The box has no top. Draw the sides to finish the pattern for the box.

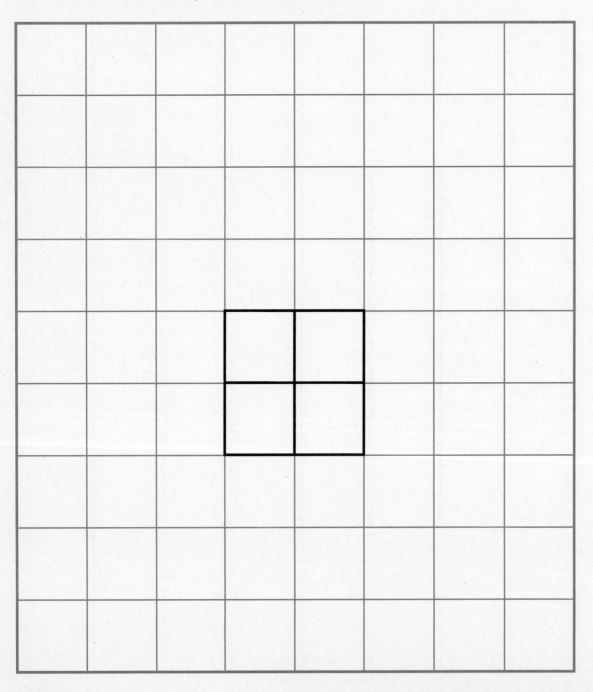

Making Boxes from the Bottom Up (page 3 of 4)

The dark squares make the bottom of a rectangular box that contains exactly 30 cubes. The box has no top. Draw the sides to finish the pattern for the box.

Making Boxes from the Bottom Up (page 4 of 4)

The dark squares make the bottom of a rectangular box that contains exactly 24 cubes. The box has no top. Draw the sides to finish the pattern for the box.

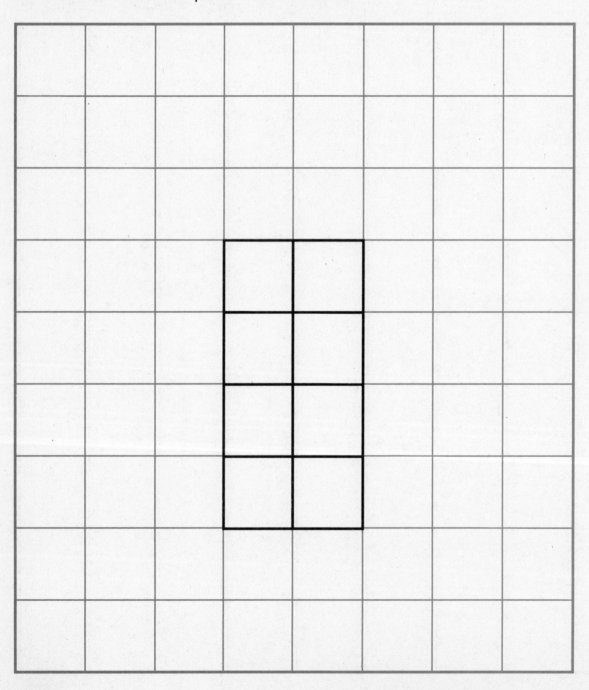

Comparing Fractions

NOTE Students compare the value of different fractions.

 60–61

Fill in <, >, or = to make each expression true.

1. $\dfrac{3}{4}$ _____ $\dfrac{4}{5}$

2. $\dfrac{7}{12}$ _____ $\dfrac{1}{2}$

3. $1\dfrac{2}{3}$ _____ $2\dfrac{1}{3}$

4. $\dfrac{5}{1}$ _____ $\dfrac{1}{5}$

5. $\dfrac{2}{12}$ _____ $\dfrac{1}{6}$

6. $\dfrac{2}{5}$ _____ $\dfrac{4}{6}$

7. $\dfrac{9}{12}$ _____ $\dfrac{7}{4}$

8. $\dfrac{0}{3}$ _____ $\dfrac{0}{8}$

A 12-Cube Box Pattern

The dark squares make the bottom of a rectangular box that contains exactly 12 cubes. The box has no top. Draw the sides to finish the pattern for the box. (Challenge: Can you find all the patterns that would make a box that holds 12 cubes?)

NOTE Students have been designing patterns for boxes (with no tops).

SMH 125–126

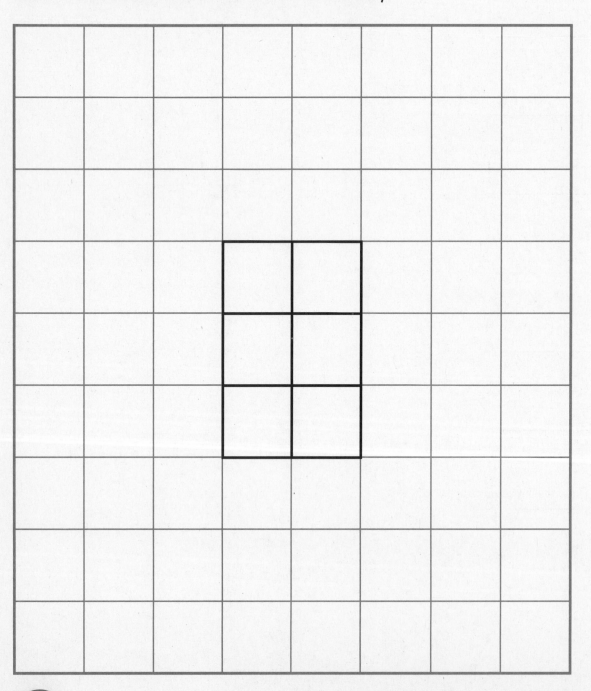

© Pearson Education 4

Moving Between Solids and Silhouettes

Finding Volume of More Boxes

How many cubes fit in each box? First, determine the answer without building the box. Then build a box and use cubes to check. For Boxes 2 and 3, also draw the pattern.

	Pattern	**Picture**	**First Answer**	**Actual Answer**
Box 1	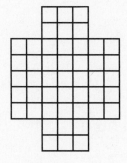		_____	_____
Box 2			_____	_____
Box 3	The bottom of the box is 4 units by 5 units. The box is 3 units high.		_____	_____

More Building Up

Use graph paper to build a pattern for the boxes described below. You may need more than one sheet of graph paper to complete the pattern.

1. The bottom of the box is 4×3, and the box will hold 36 cubes.

2. The bottom of the box is 3×3, and the box will hold 45 cubes.

3. The bottom of the box is 6×4, and the box will hold 48 cubes.

Challenge: For each problem, can you find other boxes that will hold the same number of cubes?

Double the Number of Cubes

1. You have a box that is 2 by 3 by 4. How many cubes does it hold? How do you know?

2. The factory wants you to build a box that will hold twice as many cubes. Find the dimensions of a box that contains two times as many cubes as a box that is 2 by 3 by 4. Use the space below to draw the box.

3. How many cubes will this new box contain? How do you know?

4. Is the box you found the only box that works? How do you know?

Challenge: See how many boxes you can find that will hold two times as many cubes as a 2 by 3 by 4 box. Show them on a separate sheet of paper.

A Method for Finding Volume

1. Describe a way to determine how many cubes will fit in a rectangular box. Your method should work for any box, whether you start with a box pattern, a picture of the box, or a description of the box in words.

2. Find the number of cubes that fit in a box that is 20 units by 10 units on the bottom and 12 units high. How can you convince your classmates that your answer is correct?

Portion Puzzles

Solve each problem.

NOTE Students find the total amount given the number of fractional parts.

 SMH 62

1. How many pies are needed for 12 people to each have $\frac{1}{6}$ of a pie?

2. How many pizzas are needed for 24 people to each have $\frac{1}{4}$ of a pizza?

3. How many sheets of paper are needed for 4 people to each have $3\frac{1}{4}$ sheets?

Finding the Number of Cubes

NOTE Students have been designing patterns for boxes and finding the volume of these boxes. Allow them to use their own strategies for finding the volume of this box.

SMH 125–126

1. How many unit cubes are in this package?

unit cube

Use the grid on the next page to draw a pattern for this package. Your pattern for the box should completely cover all but the top of the package. The package should completely fill the box.

2. Now how many cubes do you think are in the package?

All Kinds of Boxes

These patterns make open boxes:

NOTE Students determine the volume of boxes from 2-dimensional patterns.

 125–126

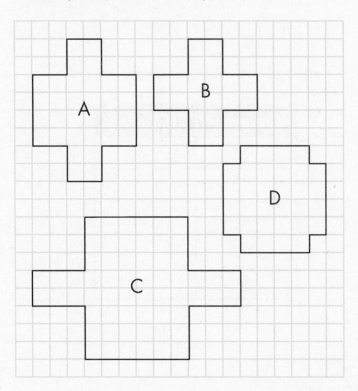

1. Which holds the greatest number of cubes? _____

2. Which box is tallest? _____ Which box is shortest? _____

Ongoing Review

3. How many cubes like the one shown would fit in a box with this pattern?

A. 26   **B.** 14   **C.** 12   **D.** 6

Converting Weights and Masses

In Problems 1 and 2, write the missing number in the blank.
Then complete the table.

1. 1 pound = _____ ounces   **2.** 1 kilogram = _____ grams

Pounds	Ounces
1	
2	
3	
4	64
5	

Kilograms	Grams
1	
2	
3	3,000
4	
5	

In Problems 3–7, convert the weights and masses.

3. 8 pounds = _____ ounces   **4.** 9 kilograms = _____ grams

5. 13 kilograms = _____ grams **6.** 20 pounds = _____ ounces

7. 3 pounds 9 ounces = _____ ounces

8. Which is heavier, 7 pounds or 160 ounces? How do you know?

_____

9. Which is greater, 20 kilograms or 2,000 grams? How do you know?

_____

More Conversions

In Problems 1 and 2, write the missing number in the blank.
Then complete the table.

1. 1 liter = _____ milliliters

Liters	Milliliters
1	
2	
3	
4	4,000
5	

2. 1 minute = _____ seconds

Minutes	Seconds
1	
2	
3	180
4	
5	

In Problems 3–11, convert each capacity or time.

3. 8 liters = _____ milliliters

4. 6 minutes = _____ seconds

5. 5 gallons = _____ quarts

6. 10 pints = _____ cups

7. 10 hours = _____ minutes

8. 25 liters = _____ milliliters

9. 7 quarts = _____ pints

10. 30 minutes = _____ seconds

11. 3 hours 15 minutes = _____ minutes

12. How many seconds are in an hour? Explain how you figured it out.

_____

Converting Measurements

Solve each riddle.

NOTE Students convert measurements from larger units to smaller units.

1. I am 1,000 times as big as a milliliter.
What am I? _____

2. I am 60 times as big as a minute.
What am I? _____

3. I am 1,000 times as big as a gram.
What am I? _____

Measurement Equivalents		
Weight and Mass		
1 pound = 16 ounces		
1 kilogram = 1,000 grams		
Capacity		
1 gallon = 4 quarts		
1 liter = 1,000 milliliters		
Time		
1 minute = 60 seconds		
1 hour = 60 minutes		

In Problems 4–10, complete each conversion.

4. 8 gallons = _____ quarts

5. 11 liters = _____ milliliters

6. 4 kilograms = _____ grams

7. 3 pounds = _____ ounces

8. 3 minutes = _____ seconds

9. 7 hours = _____ minutes

10. 8 minutes 14 seconds = _____ seconds

11. Circle the greater capacity.   8,000 milliliters   12 liters

Measurement Problems

Solve each problem and show your solution.

1. Lucy bought 3 quarts of chocolate milk and 2 gallons of white milk. How many quarts of milk did Lucy buy in all?

2. The mass of a rabbit is 4 kilograms. The mass of a mouse is 45 grams. How much greater is the mass of the rabbit?

3. Noemi poured 1.2 liters of water into a 3-liter pot. How much more water should be added to completely fill the pot?

4. There are $2\frac{1}{2}$ pints of apple juice and $1\frac{1}{2}$ pints of grape juice in the refrigerator. How much juice is there in all?

5. Mr. Dakarian bought 3 quarts of orange juice. If his family drinks 3 cups of orange juice each day, how many days will the orange juice last?

Time Problems

Solve each problem and show your work.

1. Ramona went on a long hike. She started her hike at 8:00 A.M. and hiked for 2 hours 45 minutes. When did Ramona finish her hike?

2. A television station ran a 2-minute commercial about pet food. It was followed by a 90-second commercial about an airline. Which commercial was longer? How much longer was it?

3. A party started at 7:30 P.M. and ended at 9:45 P.M. How long did the party last?

4. Mr. Chin wants to get 8 hours of sleep. If he needs to get up at 6:15 A.M., when should he go to sleep?

5. Ms. Curtis is driving 5 hours to visit her aunt. She drove for $\frac{2}{5}$ of the time and then stopped for lunch. For how many hours has she already driven?

More Measurement Problems

Solve each problem and show your work.

> **NOTE** Students use the four operations to solve problems involving measurements.

1. Marisol used $2\frac{3}{4}$ gallons of paint to paint the walls of her bedroom and $\frac{3}{4}$ of a gallon to paint the ceiling. How much paint did she use in all?

2. Jill went shopping from 3:45 P.M. to 5:00 P.M. How long did she shop?

3. The mass of a melon is 2 kilograms. The mass of a plum is 75 grams. How much greater is the mass of the melon? (1 kilogram = 1,000 grams)

4. Bill went to the museum at 11:30 A.M. He stayed for $3\frac{1}{2}$ hours. When did he leave?

5. Terrell made 4 pints of soup. How many 2-cup servings of soup would this be? (1 pint = 2 cups)

More Measurement Conversions

NOTE Students convert measurements from larger units to smaller units.

In Problems 1–4, write the missing number in the blank. Then complete the table.

1. 1 liter = _____ milliliters

Liters	Milliliters
3	3,000
4	
5	
9	
20	

2. 1 hour = _____ minutes

Hours	Minutes
4	240
5	
6	
10	
12	

3. 1 kilogram = _____ grams

Kilograms	Grams
2	2,000
3	
5	
8	
15	

4. 1 pound = _____ ounces

Pounds	Ounces
3	48
6	
8	128
10	
20	

Solving Measurement Problems

NOTE Students use the four operations to solve problems involving measurements.

Solve each problem and show your work.

1. A large canned ham has a mass of 3 kilograms. A small canned ham has a mass of 1.5 kilograms. What is the total mass of the two canned hams?

2. Mrs. Corelli worked in her garden from 1:30 P.M. to 3:15 P.M. How long did she work in her garden?

3. How many 5-minute cartoons can be shown in one hour? (The cartoons are shown one at a time.)

4. Enrique used $3\frac{1}{2}$ gallons of apple juice and $2\frac{1}{2}$ gallons of orange juice to make some fruit punch for a school picnic. How many quarts of juice are in the punch?

5. One fish bowl holds 10 liters of water and another holds 7,500 milliliters of water. Which fish bowl holds more water? How much more? (1 liter = 1,000 milliliters)

American Landmarks

Identify the silhouettes of the American symbols and landmarks listed below.

NOTE Students solve real-world problems involving the math content of this unit.

SMH 122–123

White House	Lincoln Memorial	Empire State Building
Liberty Bell	Gateway Arch	Statue of Liberty
The Alamo	Golden Gate Bridge	
Mississippi Riverboat	The Space Needle	

a.

_____

b.

_____

c.

_____

d.

_____

e.

_____

f.

_____

g.

_____

h.

_____

i.

_____

j.

_____

Polished Spiral Karin Kuhlmann

"Although the creation of fractals is bounded to strict mathematical rules, the results are always very inspiring." – **Karin Kuhlmann**

Student Activity Book

How Many Packages? How Many Groups?   UNIT 8

Investigations
IN NUMBER, DATA, AND SPACE®

How Many Packages?
How Many Groups?

Closest Estimate

Each problem below has a choice of three estimates. Which one do you think is closest? Circle the closest estimate. Then write about why you think this estimate is the closest.

1. The closest estimate for 78 × 7 is: 200   500   700
   I think this is closest because:

2. The closest estimate for 18 × 26 is: 400   600   1,000
   I think this is closest because:

3. The closest estimate for 32 × 54 is: 500   1,000   1,500
   I think this is closest because:

4. Choose one or more of the problems above and solve it to get an exact answer. Show your solution with equations. Did you choose the closest estimate?

Name _____ Date _____

How Many Packages? How Many Groups?   Daily Practice

Stamp Collections

NOTE Students practice solving addition and subtraction problems in a story problem context.

SMH 8–9, 13–15

1. Helena has a collection of stamps. She has 734 South American stamps and 555 African stamps.

   a. How many stamps does Helena have?

   b. How many more stamps does she need to have a total of 1,500 stamps?

2. Terrell also has a stamp collection. He has 839 stamps from Africa and 472 stamps from North America.

   a. How many stamps does Terrell have?

   b. How many more stamps does he need to have a total of 1,500 stamps?

3. How many more stamps does Terrell have in his collection than Helena has in her collection?

More or Less?

Without actually solving each problem, decide whether the answer to each problem is more or less than each of the landmark numbers below the problem. Answer "yes" or "no" on the line next to each question.

NOTE Students practice estimation strategies that include rounding to landmark numbers and using what they know about multiplication facts and multiplying by a multiple of 10.

1. 28×4

More than 100? _____

More than 200? _____

2. 30×13

More than 300? _____

More than 600? _____

3. 26×43

More than 500? _____

More than 1,000? _____

Less than 1,500? _____

4. Choose one of the problems above and make a close estimate. Write about how you made your estimate, including what numbers you used to help you estimate.

Name _____   Date _____

How Many Packages? How Many Groups?

Solving 2-Digit Multiplication Problems (page 1 of 2)

First, write a story to go with each problem. Then, solve the problem and show your solution. You may use arrays or pictures if they help show your strategy more clearly.

1. $53 \times 24 =$ _____

Story problem:

Solution:

© Pearson Education 4

How Many Packages? How Many Groups?

Solving 2-Digit Multiplication Problems (page 2 of 2)

2. $46 \times 37 =$ _____

Story problem:

Solution:

Multiplying Two Ways

NOTE Students solve the same 2-digit multiplication problem in two different ways.

SMH **40–41, 42**

1. Solve this problem in two different ways. Be sure to show how you got your answer.

   $31 \times 27 =$ _____

   First way:

   Second way:

Ongoing Review

2. What is the closest estimate of 39×22?

   A. 400　　**B.** 600　　**C.** 800　　**D.** 1,000

Solving a Multiplication Problem

NOTE Students use multiplication strategies that include breaking a problem apart to make smaller problems that are easier to multiply.

SMH **40–41, 42**

First, write a story problem for 22 × 34. Then, solve the problem and show how you solved it. You may include arrays or pictures of groups.

$22 \times 34 =$ _____

Story problem:

Here's how I solved it:

Two Cluster Problems

Solve the first three problems in each cluster. Show your strategy for solving the final problem. Put a star next to any of the problems in the cluster that helped you.

Set A

Solve these problems:

$4 \times 3 =$

$50 \times 3 =$

$54 \times 10 =$

Now solve $54 \times 13 =$

Set B

Solve these problems:

$2 \times 38 =$

$4 \times 38 =$

$40 \times 38 =$

Now solve $42 \times 38 =$

Name _____   Date _____

How Many Packages? How Many Groups?   **Daily Practice**

Adding Two Ways

1. Solve this problem in two different ways.
Be sure to show how you got your answer.

> **NOTE** Students use different strategies to solve addition problems. They work on efficiency and flexibility by solving the same problem in two different ways.
>
> **SMH** 8–9

$1,018 + 879 =$ _____

First way:

Second way:

Ongoing Review

2. $566 + 200 - 20 =$ _____

     A. 786   **B.** 766   **C.** 746   **D.** 546

Multiplication Cluster Problems (page 1 of 2)

In Sets A–F, solve the first three problems in each cluster.
Show your strategy for solving the final problem. Put a star
next to any of the problems in the cluster that helped you.

Set A

Solve these problems:

$6 \times 30 =$

$3 \times 30 =$

$30 \times 30 =$

Now solve $36 \times 33 =$

Set B

Solve these problems:

$7 \times 25 =$

$20 \times 25 =$

$40 \times 25 =$

Now solve $47 \times 25 =$

Set C

Solve these problems:

$3 \times 5 =$

$3 \times 60 =$

$40 \times 60 =$

Now solve $43 \times 65 =$

Multiplication Cluster Problems (page 2 of 2)

Set D

Solve these problems:

$2 \times 57 =$

$4 \times 57 =$

$40 \times 57 =$

Now solve $44 \times 57 =$

Set E

Solve these problems:

$6 \times 25 =$

$60 \times 6 =$

$60 \times 20 =$

Now solve $64 \times 26 =$

Set F

Solve these problems:

$10 \times 45 =$

$9 \times 45 =$

$4 \times 45 =$

Now solve $94 \times 45 =$

Showing Solutions with Arrays

Choose one of the problems from the two previous pages, and write it on this sheet. In the space below, draw an array to show how you can break the problem into easier problems to solve it. Remember to label the dimensions of the array and the products in each part of the array.

Problem: _____

1. Here is one way to show the solution with an array:

CHALLENGE: Show a second way.

Pencil Problems (page 1 of 2)

Read each of the story problems below, and answer each part of the problem. Show your solutions.

1. Lakeside School has 500 students. The principal orders 22 boxes of pencils. Each box has 24 pencils. Will he have enough pencils to give one to each student in the school? Write an estimate and explain your thinking.

   a. How many pencils are there in 22 boxes? Show your solution.

   b. How many more or less than 500 is that?

Pencil Problems (page 2 of 2)

2. The Park City Children's Museum needs 1,000 pencils
for its store. The museum orders pencils in boxes of 48.
Will there be enough pencils if the museum orders
25 boxes? Write an estimate and explain your thinking.

   a. How many pencils are there in 25 boxes?
   Show your solution.

   b. How many more or less than 1,000 is that?

Subtracting Two Ways

1. Solve this problem in two different ways.
Be sure to show how you got your answer.

> **NOTE** Students use strategies to solve subtraction problems. They work on efficiency and flexibility by solving the same problem in two different ways.
>
> **SMH** 13–15

$$\$30.50 - \$17.79 = \underline{\hspace{2cm}}$$

First way:

Second way:

Ongoing Review

2. $32 \times 6 = \underline{\hspace{2cm}}$

    A. 182   **B.** 186   **C.** 192   **D.** 300

Name _____ Date _____

How Many Packages? How Many Groups?   Daily Practice

Multiplication Story Problem

NOTE Students make an estimate and solve a multiplication story problem.

SMH 40–41, 42

1. The school cafeteria serves 700 students during lunch. The disposable trays come in boxes of 36. Will there be enough trays if there are 21 boxes? Write an estimate and explain your thinking.

   a. How many trays are in 21 boxes? Show your solution.

   b. How many more or less than 700 is that?

Ongoing Review

2. Which number is **not** a factor of 810?

   A. 405   **B.** 27   **C.** 25   **D.** 3

Problems About Oranges

Solve each story problem. Show your solution.
You may include arrays or pictures of groups.

NOTE Students practice multiplying 2-digit numbers by 2-digit numbers.

 40–41, 42

1. The Sunshine Fruit Company sells oranges in boxes that hold 72 oranges. Sally Green ordered 35 boxes for her grocery store. How many oranges does Ms. Green have to sell?

2. A fruit stand worker sells bags of oranges. There are 18 oranges in a bag. Over the weekend, the fruit stand worker sold 74 bags. How many oranges did he sell?

Making an Easier Problem

1. Solve these two problems and show your strategy.

   a. $15 \times 29 =$ **b.** $38 \times 16 =$

2. Read the story below and compare it to the problems above. How would you finish Sophia's and George's strategies?

   The fourth grade is selling oranges to raise money for charity. The oranges come in two sizes of boxes. The large boxes contain 29 oranges each. The small boxes contain 16 oranges each.

   a. Sophia counts up how many large boxes the class sold and counts 15 boxes. To find out how many oranges there are in total in the large boxes, Sophia first multiplies 15 and 30.

   What does Sophia have to do to finish the problem?

   b. George counts up how many small boxes the class sold and counts 38 boxes. Like Sophia, he starts with an easier problem, multiplying 40 and 16.

   What does George have to do to find how many oranges there are in total in the 38 small boxes?

Related Problems

Solve each set of problems below. Show your strategy for
the last problem in each set.

1. $7 \times 30 =$ This is how I solved 7×29:

   $7 \times 29 =$

2. $20 \times 25 =$ This is how I solved 18×25:

   $18 \times 25 =$

3. $3 \times 50 =$ This is how I solved 30×49:

   $30 \times 50 =$

   $30 \times 49 =$

4. $6 \times 22 =$ This is how I solved 59×22:

   $60 \times 22 =$

   $59 \times 22 =$

Name _____   Date _____

How Many Packages? How Many Groups?   **Daily Practice**

Coin Jars

NOTE Students solve problems about combinations of coins.

1. Damian has a coin jar full of pennies, dimes, nickels, and quarters. Most of the coins in his jar are pennies. He knows that there is $7.00 in his coin jar. What combination of coins could be in Damian's coin jar that would equal $7.00?

First solution: Second solution:

2. Ursula also has a coin jar. There are only two kinds of coins in her coin jar. She knows that there is $3.75 in her jar. What combination of coins could be in Ursula's coin jar that would equal $3.75?

First solution: Second solution:

Ongoing Review

3. $700 \times 6 =$ _____

    A. 42   **B.** 420   **C.** 4,200   **D.** 42,000

More Related Problems

Solve each pair of problems below. Show
your strategy for the second problem in
each problem.

> **NOTE** Students practice solving
> problems in which one factor is 1
> or 2 away from a multiple of 10.
> Sometimes it is helpful to solve
> problems like these by changing
> that factor to a nearby multiple
> of 10 and adjusting the answer.
>
> **SMH** 40–43

1. $14 \times 20 =$ This is how I solved
$14 \times 19 =$ 14×19:

2. $30 \times 25 =$ This is how I solved 28×25:
$28 \times 25 =$

3. $35 \times 30 =$ This is how I solved 35×29:
$35 \times 29 =$

4. $50 \times 40 =$ This is how I solved 50×38:
$50 \times 38 =$

More Multiplication Cluster Problems (page 1 of 2)

In Sets A–D, solve each set of problems. Show your strategy for the problem in the second column.

Set A

Solve these problems:

$30 \times 50 =$

$7 \times 50 =$

$37 \times 2 =$

$3 \times 52 =$

$30 \times 52 =$

Now solve $37 \times 52 =$

Set B

Solve these problems:

$6 \times 6 =$

$60 \times 60 =$

$60 \times 63 =$

$63 \times 60 =$

$3 \times 63 =$

Now solve $63 \times 63 =$

More Multiplication
Cluster Problems (page 2 of 2)

Set C

Solve these problems: | Now solve $59 \times 93 =$

$50 \times 90 =$

$60 \times 90 =$

$9 \times 90 =$

$59 \times 90 =$

$59 \times 3 =$

Set D

Solve these problems: | Now solve $85 \times 26 =$

$8 \times 25 =$

$8 \times 26 =$

$80 \times 26 =$

$85 \times 10 =$

$85 \times 20 =$

Making Cluster Problems (page 1 of 2)

Estimate the answer to each problem. Make up a cluster of problems to help you solve each problem. Exchange clusters with a partner and solve each other's clusters.

1. $39 \times 75 =$ Estimate: _____

2. $44 \times 28 =$ Estimate: _____

How Many Packages? How Many Groups?

Making Cluster Problems (page 2 of 2)

3. $64 \times 73 =$ Estimate: _____

4. $58 \times 46 =$ Estimate: _____

More Problems About Oranges

Solve each story problem below. Show your solutions.
You may also show your solutions with arrays or pictures
of groups.

1. Annie has filled her delivery truck with 70 boxes of
   oranges. Each box contains 50 oranges. When she gets
   to the supermarket, the grocer wants only 68 boxes. She
   decides to take the extra boxes to the food bank.

   a. How many oranges does Annie have on the truck?

   b. How many oranges does the grocer want?

   c. How many oranges will Annie give the food bank?

2. Jim is packing oranges into boxes that are meant to
   hold 50 oranges. But the oranges are too big! He can
   only fit 49 oranges into each box. He has 36 boxes to
   fill. How many oranges will he need?

Daily Practice

Addition and Subtraction

Solve the problems below. Show your solutions, using clear and concise notation.

NOTE Students practice solving addition and subtraction problems.

SMH 8–9, 13–15

1.   536
     + 647

2.   724
     − 248

3. 851 + 463 = _____

4.   1,250
     − 629

5. _____ + 842 = 1,600

6. 1,200 − _____ = 350

7. _____ + 712 = 1,350

8. 800 − _____ = 499

Name _____   Date _____

How Many Packages? How Many Groups?   **Daily Practice**

Solving Another Multiplication Problem

NOTE Students solve a 2-digit multiplication problem.

SMH 40–43

Write a story problem for 65 × 35. Then solve the problem and show how you solved it.

1. 65 × 35 = _____

Story problem:

Here is how I solved it:

Ongoing Review

2. Which number is **not** a factor of 750?

     A. 250   **B.** 75   **C.** 15   **D.** 7

Division Practice

Solve each division problem below. Then write the related multiplication combination.

NOTE Students review division problems that are related to known multiplication combinations.

 35

Division Problem	Multiplication Combination
1. 63 ÷ 7 = _____	_____ × _____ = _____
2. 72 ÷ 9 = _____	_____ × _____ = _____
3. 56 ÷ 8 = _____	_____ × _____ = _____
4. 64 ÷ 8 = _____	_____ × _____ = _____
5. 121 ÷ 11 = _____	_____ × _____ = _____
6. 84 ÷ 7 = _____	_____ × _____ = _____
7. 48 ÷ 6 = _____	_____ × _____ = _____
8. 36 ÷ 4 = _____	_____ × _____ = _____
9. $6\overline{)42}$	_____ × _____ = _____
10. $9\overline{)54}$	_____ × _____ = _____

Multiplying 4-Digit Numbers by 1-Digit Numbers (page 1 of 2)

Solve each problem and show your work.

1. 1,548 students attend the Sunset Elementary School. The principal wants to make sure each student gets 5 pencils to start the school year. How many pencils does she need to buy?

2. The Fresh Fruit Company can fit 2,650 oranges in one truck. One day they sent out 3 trucks full of oranges to deliver the fruit to grocery stores. How many oranges did they send out that day?

3. $2,124 \times 4 =$

4. $3,670 \times 9 =$

How Many Packages? How Many Groups?

Multiplying 4-Digit Numbers by 1-Digit Numbers (page 2 of 2)

Solve each problem and show your work.

5. There are 6 schools in town. Each school serves 1,409 lunches each week. How many lunches are served by the schools in the town each week?

6. Seven truck drivers each drove 4,215 miles in a two-week period. How many miles did they drive in all?

7. $8,437 \times 2 =$

8. $4,750 \times 8 =$

Driving Around

Ms. Ortega drives her truck to different cities throughout the year. The table shows the roundtrip distance to each city and how many times she made each trip last year. For each city in the table, show the total number of miles Ms. Ortega drove.

> **NOTE** Students multiply 4-digit numbers by 1-digit numbers.

Use the space below the table to show your work.

City	Roundtrip Distance	Number of Trips	Total Number of Miles
Lincoln, NE	1,448	3	
Gainesville, FL	1,850	6	
Seattle, WA	3,528	8	
Sacramento, CA	2,922	5	

How Many Legs?

Solve these problems and show your work.

NOTE Students multiply 4-digit numbers by 1-digit numbers.

How many legs do ...

1. 4,366 children have? _____

2. 2,066 spiders have? (A spider has 8 legs.) _____

3. 3,219 dogs have? _____

4. 1,077 three-legged stools have? _____

5. 5,910 beetles have? (A beetle has 6 legs.) _____

Writing Multiplication
Story Problems (page 1 of 2)

Write a story problem for each problem. Then solve the
problem and show your solution.

1. 28 × 53 = _____

   Story problem:

   Solution:

2. 83 × 19 = _____

   Story problem:

   Solution:

Writing Multiplication Story Problems (page 2 of 2)

3. $55 \times 74 =$ _____

Story problem:

Solution:

4. $67 \times 46 =$ _____

Story problem:

Solution:

"How Far?" Problems

Solve the following problems and explain how you found the distance between the numbers.

NOTE Students use addition and subtraction to solve problems.

SMH 13–15

1. How far is it from 752 to 1,000?

2. How far is it from 619 to 2,000?

3. How far is it from 1,345 to 3,000?

4. How far is it from 4,658 to 5,000?

Ongoing Review

5. 8 is a factor of which number?

   A. 50   **B.** 300   **C.** 400   **D.** 500

Selling Fruit

NOTE Students practice solving addition and subtraction problems in a story problem context.

SMH 8–9, 13–15

1. On Monday, a grocery store received a shipment of 1,000 apples. The apples were quite tasty, and the store sold 346 of them that day. How many apples were left to sell the next day?

2. On Wednesday, the store received a shipment of 1,200 oranges. The store sold 263 oranges that day. How many oranges were left to sell the next day?

3. On Saturday, the store received a shipment of 2,000 mangos. The store sold 415 mangos on Saturday and 680 mangos on Sunday.

a. How many mangos did the store sell on the weekend (Saturday and Sunday)?

b. How many mangos were left to sell on Monday morning?

© Pearson Education 4

Solving Division Problems

Solve the story problems below. Write an equation for each problem and show how you solved it so that someone else reading this will understand your thinking.

NOTE Students review the meaning of division problems and practice solving them.

SMH 44, 50–52

1. Marco wants to sell his marble collection at a yard sale. He has 112 marbles that he wants to put in bags with 8 marbles in each bag. How many bags of marbles will he have?

Equation:

Solution:

2. Marco baked 96 cookies to sell at the yard sale. He wants to fill 6 cookie tins with the same number of cookies in each tin. How many cookies should he put in each tin?

Equation:

Solution:

Problems About Teams (page 1 of 2)

Solve each of the story problems and show your solutions. You may also use a picture to explain your thinking.

1. It is field day at Riverside School. All of the fourth graders are outside playing games. There are 126 students. Each team has 14 students. How many teams can they make?

2. There are 112 students in third grade. How many teams of 7 can they make?

3. There are 120 students in fifth grade. How many teams of 15 can they make?

Problems About Teams (page 2 of 2)

4. There are 95 students in second grade. How many teams of 5 can they make?

5. There are 154 students in sixth grade. How many teams of 11 can they make?

6. There are 132 students in first grade. How many teams of 6 can they make?

Name   Date

How Many Packages? How Many Groups?   **Daily Practice**

How Many Hundreds? How Many Total?

NOTE Students estimate and solve addition problems.

SMH 8–9

1. Here are the numbers of postcards in six collections.

74, 46, 98, 22, 113, 51

   a. About how many hundreds of postcards are there in all?

      Estimate: 300 or 400 or 500 or 600?
How did you decide?

   b. Add the numbers to find the exact total number of postcards.

2. Here are the costs of 4 items at the grocery store.
$1.31, $2.71, $1.97, $3.04

   a. About how much do the 4 items cost?

      Estimate: $7.00 or $8.00 or $9.00 or $10.00?
How did you decide?

   b. Add the numbers to find the exact cost of the 4 items.

Ongoing Review

3. What is 300 more than 2,816?

   A. 5,816   **B.** 3,116   **C.** 2,516   **D.** 2,116

Multiplication Practice

Solve each problem in two ways. Record your solutions.

NOTE Students practice solving 2-digit multiplication problems. They have been working on breaking numbers apart in a variety of ways in order to solve these problems.

 40–43

1. $63 \times 45 =$ _____

First way:

Second way:

2. $72 \times 56 =$ _____

First way:

Second way:

Marvin's Mystery Multiple Tower

This is the top part of Marvin's multiple tower:

| 240 |
| 224 |
| 208 |
| 192 |
| 176 |

1. By what number is Marvin counting?

2. How many numbers are in Marvin's tower so far?
How do you know?

3. What is Marvin's 10th multiple?

4. If Marvin adds 5 more numbers to his tower, on what
number will he land?

Problems About Multiple Towers (page 1 of 2)

1. This is the top part of Malia's multiple tower.

299
276
253
230
207

a. By what number is Malia counting?

b. What is Malia's 10th multiple?
How do you know?

c. What is her 20th multiple?
How do you know?

2. This is the top part of Marco's multiple tower.

198
180
162
144
126

a. By what number is Marco counting?

b. What is Marco's 5th multiple?
How do you know?

c. What will his 15th multiple be?
How do you know?

Problems About Multiple Towers (page 2 of 2)

3. This is the top part of Megan's multiple tower.

360
345
330
315
300

a. By what number is Megan counting?

b. How many numbers are in Megan's tower? How do you know?

c. What is her 10th multiple? How do you know?

4. This is the top part of Michael's multiple tower.

651
620
589
558
527

a. By what number is Michael counting?

b. How many numbers are in Michael's tower? How do you know?

c. What will his 25th multiple be? How do you know?

Solving Division Problems (page 1 of 2)

Solve each problem. You may want to represent the problem with pictures. Show your solutions.

1. You have 3 decks of cards with 52 cards in each deck. How many cards will each person get if the 3 decks are dealt out evenly to 6 people?

2. Cans of juice come in cases of 24. How many cases do you need to give one can to each of 264 students?

3. A lunar month (from the day of the new moon to the day of the next new moon) is about 28 days. About how many lunar months are in a year (365 days)?

How Many Packages? How Many Groups?

Solving Division Problems (page 2 of 2)

4. $16\overline{)256}$

5. $508 \div 22 = $ _____

6. $360 \div 11 = $ _____

Name _____ Date _____

How Many Packages? How Many Groups?   **Daily Practice**

Reading a Long Book

NOTE Students practice solving addition and subtraction problems in a story problem context.

SMH 8, 9, 13–15

1. Noemi borrowed a new book from the library. At 1,000 pages, it is the longest book she has ever tried to read! Today, she read 115 pages. How many more pages does she have to read to reach the end?

2. In the next week, Noemi reads 388 more pages. How many pages has she read in all?

3. At the end of 2 weeks, Noemi has read 816 pages. How many pages does she have left to finish the book?

Ongoing Review

4. How many 1,000s are in 7,010?

   A. 7   **B.** 70   **C.** 700   **D.** 7,000

© Pearson Education 4

Name _____ Date _____

How Many Packages? How Many Groups?   Daily Practice

Solving a Division Story Problem

NOTE Students solve a division problem in a story context.

 46, 52

1. Ms. Kim's class has 185 books in their classroom library. She puts 45 books on each shelf.

   a. How many shelves have 45 books?

   b. How many books are on the last shelf?

Ongoing Review

2. What is the next multiple in this multiple tower?

   A. 180   **B.** 189   **C.** 191   **D.** 193

162
135
108
81

Writing a Division Story Problem

> **NOTE** Students have been working on solving division problems with 2-digit and 3-digit numbers. It is often helpful to think of a division problem in a story context.
>
> **SMH** 46, 50, 51, 52

1. Choose one of the division problems below and circle it. Write a story problem to go with it. Then solve the division problem, and show your solution. (You may do more than one problem if you have time.)

$$96 \div 12 = \qquad 135 \div 9 = \qquad 169 \div 13 =$$

Story problem:

Solution:

Ongoing Review

2. Richard had $6.47. He spent $4.28 on a poster. How much money does Richard have left?

A. $10.75   **B.** $2.29   **C.** $2.19   **D.** $1.19

Jill's Multiple Tower

This is the top part of Jill's multiple tower.

NOTE Students solve problems involving multiples.

 36

432
405
378
351
324

1. By what number is Jill counting?

2. How many numbers are in Jill's tower so far? How do you know?

3. What is Jill's 10th multiple?

4. Imagine that Jill adds more multiples to her tower. What would be the 20th multiple in her tower? How do you know?

Ongoing Review

5. What is the closest estimate of 375 ÷ 23?

A. 10   **B.** 15   **C.** 30   **D.** 150

Division Problems About Pencils

NOTE Students practice understanding story problems and solving division problems.

SMH 48–49, 50–52

Solve each problem below and show your solutions. You need these two pieces of information for these problems.

- Pencils come in packages of 12.
- There are 23 students in Mr. Coburn's class.

1. How many packages of pencils does Mr. Coburn have to open to give 2 pencils to everyone in his class?

2. How many packages of pencils does Mr. Coburn have to open to give 4 pencils to everyone in his class?

3. How many packages of pencils does Mr. Coburn have to open to give 6 pencils to everyone in his class?

Dividing 4-Digit Numbers
by 1-Digit Numbers (page 1 of 2)

Solve each problem and show your work.

1. In one day at Honeysweet Apple Orchard, workers
picked 1,549 apples. They want to put them in
bags of 6. How many bags can they make?

2. 1,004 children signed up to play in the Smith City youth
basketball league. 8 children will be placed on each
team. How many teams of 8 players will there be?

3. $2,831 \div 5 =$

4. $5,346 \div 7 =$

Dividing 4-Digit Numbers by 1-Digit Numbers (page 2 of 2)

Solve each problem and show your work.

5. 1,452 shirts were delivered to a large department store. They came in boxes of 4. How many boxes were delivered?

6. 3,018 letters need to be mailed out to members of the City Service Club. Five people are stuffing the envelopes. How should they divide up the task so that each person will stuff the same number of envelopes?

7. $4,698 \div 9 =$

8. $2,287 \div 3 =$

Dividing Large Numbers

Solve each problem and show your work.

NOTE Students divide 4-digit numbers by 1-digit numbers.

1. A football stadium has 4,890 seats. There are 6 sections of seats with the same number of seats in each section. How many seats are in each section?

2. A big company is planning to have a dinner for 1,418 people. How many tables are needed if 8 people will sit at each table?

3. $2,212 \div 7 =$

4. $4,676 \div 2 =$

Flea Market

Solve each problem and show your work.

NOTE Students divide 4-digit numbers by 1-digit numbers.

1. Mr. Diaz makes bracelets and sells them at flea markets. He uses 8 beads for each bracelet. Mr. Diaz has a bag of 1,500 beads. How many bracelets can he make?

2. Ms. Lang has a collection of 2,106 old postcards that she bought at flea markets. She stores them in 6 boxes, with the same number in each box. How many postcards are in each box?

3. $3,241 \div 7 =$

4. $6,708 \div 4 =$

Solving Multiplication and Division Problems (page 1 of 2)

For each problem below, first make a close estimate. Then solve each problem, and show your work.

1. Cory buys stickers in packages of 36 for his sticker collection. Last year, he bought 97 packages of stickers. How many stickers did he buy?

   Estimate:

   Solution:

2. Tanya has 460 sports cards in her collection, which she keeps in a binder that holds 8 cards on a page. How many pages has she filled?

   Estimate:

   Solution:

Solving Multiplication and Division Problems (page 2 of 2)

3. The city soccer league has 273 players who have signed up to play on teams. They want to make 18 teams. How many players can they put on each team?

Estimate:

Solution:

4. The fourth graders sold packages of seeds to raise money for their class trip. Each package costs $0.75. The students sold 62 packages in all. How much money did they raise?

Estimate:

Solution:

School Supplies

NOTE Students practice solving addition and subtraction problems in a story problem context.

SMH 8–9, 13–15

1. Mr. Mancillas had $200 to spend on art supplies. He spent $103.80 on drawing paper and $86.35 on paintbrushes.

   a. How much did he spend on art supplies?

   b. How much money did he have left after he bought the supplies?

2. Ms. Kim had $300 to spend on science supplies. She spent $77.49 on thermometers and $212.99 on a microscope.

   a. How much did she spend on science materials?

   b. How much money did she have left after she bought science materials?

Ongoing Review

3. Which of the following is true?

   A. $875 - 476 > 400$ **C.** $640 - 139 < 500$

   B. $933 - 734 < 200$ **D.** $521 - 420 < 100$

Say Cheese! (page 1 of 2)

Use the data below to solve Problems 1–3.
Show your work on another sheet of paper.

NOTE Students solve real-world problems involving the math content of this unit.

SMH 40–43, 50–52

Film	Number of pictures
PF-12	12
PF-24	24
PF-36	36

1. Mandy bought 15 rolls of PF-12 film for summer camp. How many pictures can she take?

2. Paco took 288 pictures, using rolls of PF-36 film. How many rolls did he use?

Say Cheese! (page 2 of 2)

3. Monroe School has 753 students. The Family Club is taking a picture of every student in the school. How many rolls of PF-24 will the club need to buy?

4. Sylvia has a digital camera. Instead of film, her camera uses a memory card that stores 26 pictures. When the card is filled, she transfers the pictures to her computer and uses the card again. Last summer, she took 416 pictures. How many times did Sylvia fill the memory card?

Polished Spiral Karin Kuhlmann

"Although the creation of fractals is bounded to strict mathematical rules, the results are always very inspiring." – **Karin Kuhlmann**

Investigations
IN NUMBER, DATA, AND SPACE®

Penny Jars and Plant Growth

Investigation 3

Penny Jars and Plant Growth

Plant Height Chart (page 1 of 2)

Plant Name _____

Date	Day of the Week	Height	Comments

Penny Jars and Plant Growth

Plant Height Chart (page 2 of 2)

Date	Day of the Week	Height	Comments

Temperatures in Two Cities (page 1 of 2)

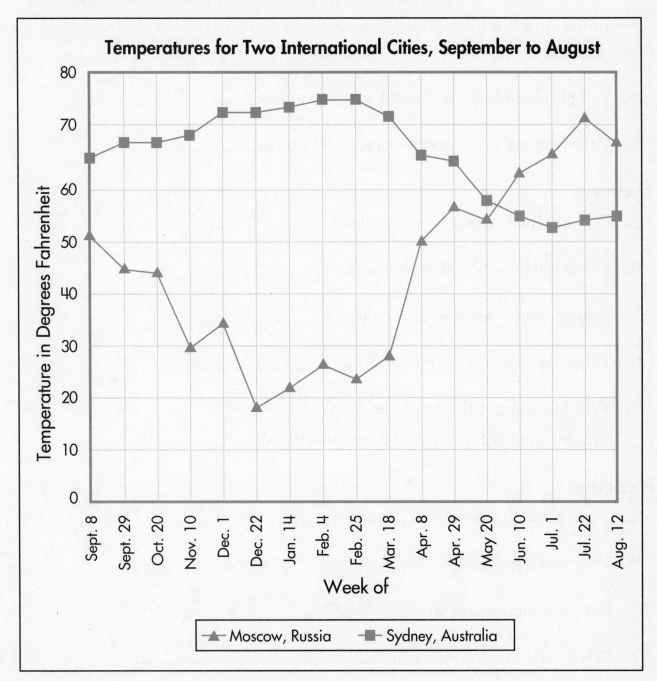

Temperatures for Two International Cities, September to August

Penny Jars and Plant Growth

Temperatures in Two Cities (page 2 of 2)

Look at the graph on the previous page to answer
these questions:

1. Which place has the hottest temperature? _____

2. Which place has the coldest temperature? _____

Sydney:

3. During which week was it hottest? _____

4. What was the hottest temperature? _____

5. During which week was it coldest? _____

6. What was the coldest temperature? _____

7. What was the difference between
   Sydney's hottest and coldest temperatures? _____

Moscow:

8. During which week was it hottest? _____

9. What was the hottest temperature? _____

10. During which week was it coldest? _____

11. What was the coldest temperature? _____

12. What was the difference between
    Moscow's hottest and coldest temperatures? _____

The Motion Graph (page 1 of 2)

This graph shows a runner's speed during a race.

1. At which point is the runner speeding up?

2. At which point has the runner stopped?

The Motion Graph (page 2 of 2)

3. At which point is the runner going at a slow, steady speed?

4. What is the runner doing at d?

5. What is the runner doing at f?

6. What is the runner doing at c?

7. What might have happened to this runner during the race? Tell the whole story on another sheet of paper.

Temperatures for a Day in June: Anchorage, Alaska

NOTE Students plot points on a graph of temperature changes.

 72, 73, 74

1. Here is a table that shows the temperature at different times during a June day in Alaska. (F stands for Fahrenheit.) Make a graph of the data on the grid below.

2. At what time is it the warmest on this day in June?

_____

3. At what time is it the coldest?

_____

Time	Temperature
3:00 A.M.	39°F
6:00 A.M.	47°F
9:00 A.M.	52°F
12:00 noon	57°F
3:00 P.M.	60°F
6:00 P.M.	58°F
9:00 P.M.	55°F
12:00 midnight	47°F

Ongoing Review

4. How does the temperature change from noon to midnight?

   A. It gets colder.

   B. It gets warmer.

   C. It gets warmer, and then colder.

   D. It stays the same.

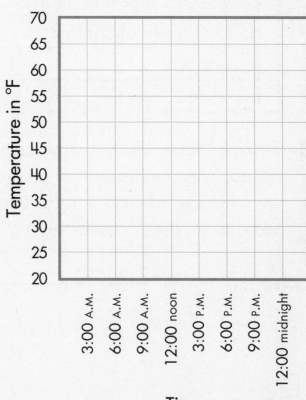

© Pearson Education 4

The Boston Marathon (page 1 of 3)

The next pages tell the story of Bobby Hall's experience racing in the Boston Marathon in a wheelchair. The underlined words in the story describe his speed and how it changed throughout the race.

1. Make a graph of the racer's speed over the course of the race.

2. Find the places on your graph where the racer is doing what the underlined words describe. Write the words on your graph in the right place.

    Here is a list of the underlined words in the story.

a. wheeled very fast	**g.** gradually slowing down
b. slowed down a bit	**h.** kept pushing slowly
c. wheeled nice and steady	**i.** picked up the pace
d. push faster and faster	**j.** ran my fastest
e. stopped	**k.** wheeled around slowly
f. wheeled steadily	

3. Some of these words and phrases describe the racer's speed. Some of them describe a **change** in speed. Sort these words and phrases into two lists. Put each word or phrase under the correct heading below.

Speed	Change in Speed

The Boston Marathon (page 2 of 3)

Participating in the Boston Marathon—all 26.2 miles of it—is an incredible experience. You're with thousands of other people, going through all kinds of different towns and cities and college campuses. Wheelchair participants get a lot of attention in Boston. People know us and they start us right at the front.

In the beginning of the race, there's about 4 miles of downhill. Like most wheelchair participants, I wheeled very fast on that downhill part. It felt good. But at mile 4, I remembered to pace myself. I slowed down a bit. For the next 9 miles or so, I wheeled nice and steady.

But then a very exciting thing happened. At Wellesley College, there was a huge crowd of students lining the course, screaming and clapping like crazy. All that excitement made me push faster and faster through the mile-long part of Wellesley. But then I noticed I was tired—too tired for being just a little more than halfway through the race. I stopped for a few seconds to get some water and pour some over my head. (I was getting hot, too!) I knew the hardest part of the race was coming up.

After Wellesley, I wheeled steadily for a few more miles. But then, by the seventeenth mile, it started getting hard. From mile 17 to 21 or so, I could feel myself gradually slowing down. There's a bunch of hard hills, and I knew I just had to take it easy to make it over those hills. My arms were aching so much. But the funny thing was, even once I had made it over the hills, I kept pushing slowly.

The Boston Marathon (page 3 of 3)

I think by 21 miles, I was running out of steam. It was hard to keep picking up my arms. Between 21 and 25 miles, I kept pushing slowly.

By 25 miles, I knew I would make it and I picked up the pace. The crowd was tremendous in the last mile or so. They just wouldn't let you slow down. The final stretch of a quarter mile or so is downhill, and I actually wheeled my fastest for that stretch. My arms felt all beaten up and shaky at the finish—but I wheeled around slowly for a while afterwards. That helps you keep from getting so stiff the next day.

—Bobby Hall (from a telephone interview)

Barney's Mystery Multiple Tower

NOTE Students find factors and multiples using a multiple tower.

SMH 36

The picture shows part of Barney's multiple tower.

1. What number is Barney counting by?

594
567
540
513
486

2. How many numbers are in Barney's tower so far? How do you know?

3. If Barney adds five more numbers to his tower, what number will he land on?

Ongoing Review

4. What is Barney's 15th multiple?

   A. 15   **B.** 275   **C.** 405   **D.** 450

Temperatures for a Day in June: El Paso, Texas

NOTE Students plot points on a graph of temperature changes.

 72–76

1. Here is a table that shows the temperature at different times during a June day in Texas. (F stands for Fahrenheit.) Make a graph of the data on the grid below.

Time	Temperature
3:00 A.M.	72°F
6:00 A.M.	70°F
9:00 A.M.	73°F
12:00 noon	80°F
3:00 P.M.	87°F
6:00 P.M.	87°F
9:00 P.M.	84°F
12:00 midnight	80°F

2. At what time is it the warmest on this day in June?

_____

3. At what time is it the coolest?

_____

4. How does the temperature change between 3:00 a.m. and midnight?

_____

_____

_____

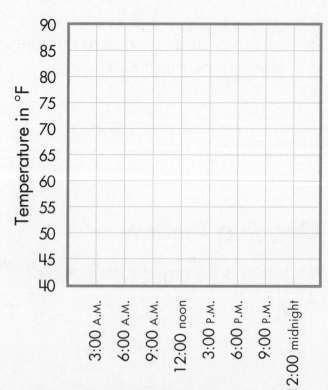

Penny Jar Amounts

1. Fill in the numbers for your first Penny Jar situation:

   a. Start with _____ pennies. Add _____ pennies each round.

   b. How many pennies are in the jar after 6 rounds?

2. Fill in the numbers for your second Penny Jar situation:

   a. Start with _____ pennies. Add _____ pennies each round.

   b. How many pennies are in the jar after 6 rounds?

A Vegetable Farm

Solve each story problem below and show
your solutions. You may also use a picture
to explain your thinking.

NOTE Students practice solving
multiplication and division problems
in story problem contexts.

SMH 45

1. Ms. Mason is packing pumpkins into crates. She has
   216 pumpkins, and each crate can hold 8 pumpkins.
   How many crates does she need?

2. Mr. Lee needs to pack potatoes. He has 24 sacks to
   pack 288 potatoes. How many potatoes can he put
   in each sack?

3. Mr. Gorton stores corn in boxes. There are 47 boxes
   with 95 ears of corn in each box. How much corn
   does he store?

A Race or Trip

NOTE In this homework, students practice making connections between a story and a graph.

SMH 75–76

1. Write a simple story about a race or trip that involves changing speeds.

2. Now sketch a line graph to show how speed changes in your story.

Closest Estimate

NOTE Students estimate products and quotients.

Circle the closest estimate.

1. $1,788 \times 4 \approx$ 700   6,000   7,000

2. $3,421 \div 6 \approx$ 500   600   700

3. $2,109 \times 5 \approx$ 10,000   12,000   100,000

4. $1,770 \times 8 \approx$ 10,000   12,000   14,000

5. $5,738 \div 3 \approx$ 190   1,900   18,000

6. $6,525 \div 9 \approx$ 700   800   900

Penny Jar Table (page 1 of 2)

1. **a.** Fill in the numbers for a Penny Jar situation:

   Start with _____ pennies. Add _____ pennies each round.

   b. Complete this table:

Number of Rounds	Total Number of Pennies
Start with	
1	
2	
3	
4	
5	
6	
7	
10	
15	
20	

Penny Jar Table (page 2 of 2)

2. How did you determine the number of pennies for round 10?

3. How did you determine the number of pennies for round 20?

Solving Division Problems

NOTE Students practice solving division problems.

SMH 50–52

Solve each problem. Show your solutions.

1. $21\overline{)352}$

2. $459 \div 17 = $ _____

3. Venetta has 405 pictures to put in an album. Each page of an album holds 12 pictures. How many pages does Venetta need for all of her pictures?

Ongoing Review

4. Which number is **not** a multiple of 24?

A. 120   **B.** 264   **C.** 300   **D.** 360

Adding Pennies to a Penny Jar 1

NOTE Students have been working with these Penny Jar situations in class. They use what they know about the start amount and the repeated change to figure out the total number of pennies at a future point.

SMH 78, 79

There are 8 pennies in the jar at the start. We add 5 pennies each round.

After 1 round there are 13 pennies.

1. How many pennies are in the jar after 2 rounds?

2. How many pennies are in the jar after 4 rounds?

3. How many pennies are in the jar after 6 rounds? How do you know?

4. Use a picture, diagram, or table to represent this Penny Jar situation in the space below.

Round 20 (page 1 of 2)

Here is a Penny Jar Situation: Start with 5 pennies.
Add 6 pennies each round.

1. Complete this table for this Penny Jar situation.

Number of Rounds	Calculation	Total Number of Pennies
5		
10		
15		
20		

2. How did you find the amount for round 20?

Round 20 (page 2 of 2) ✎ WRITING

3. Jake says that the total number of pennies for round 20 is double the number for round 10 because the double of 10 is 20. Marisol disagrees and says that Jake's method will not work. Do you agree with Jake or with Marisol? Why?

   a. Write your explanation in words.

   b. Create a representation for this Penny Jar situation that shows your ideas about whether doubling works.

Adding Pennies to a Penny Jar 2

There is 1 penny in the jar at the start.
We add 4 pennies each round.

After 1 round there are 5 pennies.

NOTE Students are using a table to record what happens in a situation of constant change. They have been working with these Penny Jar situations in class. They use what they know to figure out the total number of pennies at a future point.

SMH 78, 80

1. Complete this table to show what happens for 7 rounds.

Number of Rounds	Total Number of Pennies
Start with	
1	
2	
3	
4	
5	
6	
7	

2. How many pennies will there be in the jar after 10 rounds? How did you figure this out?

Solve in Two Ways, Multiplication

Solve each problem in two ways.
Record your solutions.

NOTE Students practice solving 2-digit multiplication problems. They work on efficiency and flexibility by solving the problem in two ways.

SMH 40–43

1. $76 \times 29 =$ _____

First way:

Second way:

2. $34 \times 88 =$ _____

First way:

Second way:

Matching Tables and Graphs (page 1 of 2)

Which table goes with Graph 1? How do you know?

Graph 1

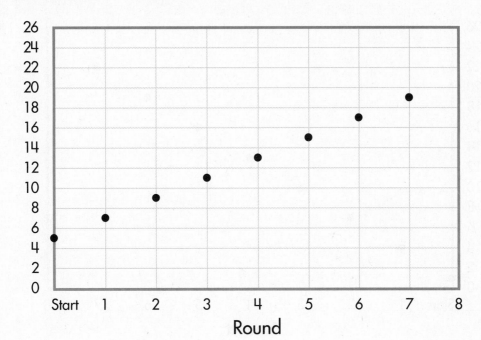

```
Tape or glue
the matching
table here.
```

Matching Tables and Graphs (page 2 of 2)

Which table goes with Graph 2? How do you know?

Graph 2

Round

Tape or glue
the matching
table here.

Graphing a Penny Jar (page 1 of 2)

Start with _____ pennies. Add _____ pennies each round.

1. Complete this table:

Number of Rounds	Total Number of Pennies
Start with	
1	
2	
3	
4	
5	
6	
7	
10	
15	
20	

2. How many pennies are there after 30 rounds? _____

3. How many pennies are there after 50 rounds? _____

4. How many pennies are there after 100 rounds? _____

5. How did you figure out the number of pennies after 100 rounds? Use number sentences to show what you did.

_____

Graphing a Penny Jar (page 2 of 2)

6. Make a graph for your Penny Jar situation.

How Many Windows?
How Many Cars?

NOTE Students practice solving multiplication and division problems.

SMH 45

Solve each problem below. Show your work.

1. There are 625 windows on Steve's apartment building. Each floor of the building has the same number of windows. If the building is 25 stories tall, how many windows are on each floor?

2. The office building next to Steve's apartment is 77 stories tall. If there are 44 windows on each floor, how many windows are there in all?

Ongoing Review

3. When the parking garage is completely full, it holds 900 cars. There are 12 levels in the garage. Each level holds the same number of cars. How many cars can be parked on each level?

   A. 15   **B.** 20   **C.** 25   **D.** 75

Penny Jar Tables (page 1 of 2)

Here are the tables for two Penny Jar situations. Complete the tables and then show how you figured out the answers to the questions.

NOTE Students fill in missing values in tables and determine values for later rounds in two Penny Jar situations.

SMH 78, 80

Table A

Number of Rounds	Total Number of Pennies
Start with	7
1	11
2	
3	
4	23
5	27
6	
7	

1. How many pennies are there after 10 rounds? _____

2. How many pennies are there after 20 rounds? _____

© Pearson Education 4

Penny Jar Tables (page 2 of 2)

Table B

Number of Rounds	Total Number of Pennies
Start with	6
1	
2	16
3	
4	26
5	
6	36
7	

3. How many pennies are there after 10 rounds? _____

4. How many pennies are there after 20 rounds? _____

Windows and Towers (page 1 of 2)

1. Fill in the table for the single tower.

Single Tower

Number of Floors	Number of Windows
1	
2	
3	
4	
5	
6	
7	
8	
9	
10	

2. **a.** How did you figure out the number of windows on 10 floors?

   b. Write an arithmetic expression that shows how you figured this out.

3. **a.** How many windows are there on 15 floors?

   b. Write an arithmetic expression that shows how you figured this out.

Windows and Towers (page 2 of 2)

4. Fill in the table for the double tower.

Double Tower

Number of Floors	Number of Windows
1	
2	
3	
4	
5	
6	
7	
8	
9	
10	

5. a. How did you figure out the number of windows on 10 floors?

   b. Write an arithmetic expression that shows how you figured this out.

6. a. How many windows are there on 15 floors?

   b. Write an arithmetic expression that shows how you figured this out.

Penny Jar Comparisons (page 1 of 3)

1. Card number: _____

2. Situation A: Start with _____ pennies. Add _____ each round.

3. Situation B: Start with _____ pennies. Add _____ each round.

4. Complete the table below:

Round	Situation A: Total Number of Pennies	Situation B: Total Number of Pennies
Starts with		
1		
2		
3		
4		
5		
6		
7		
10		
15		
20		

5. What do you notice about the table? Write your answer on another sheet of paper.

Penny Jar Comparisons (page 2 of 3)

6. Show each Penny Jar situation on the graph.
Use a different color for each situation.

© Pearson Education 4

Penny Jar Comparisons (page 3 of 3)

7. What do you notice about the graph?

_____

_____

_____

_____

_____

8. Does Penny Jar B ever have as many pennies as Penny Jar A? How do you know?

Estimate and Solve

Make an estimate for each problem. Then solve the problem. Show your solution.

> **NOTE** Students first make an estimate and then solve multiplication problems.
>
> **SMH** 40–43

1. $53 \times 71 =$

Estimate: _____

Solve:

2. $18 \times 93 =$

Estimate: _____

Solve:

3. $45 \times 55 =$

Estimate: _____

Solve:

Ongoing Review

4. What is the closest estimate for $420 \div 15$?

A. 20   **B.** 30   **C.** 40   **D.** 42

Your Own Penny Jar

Make up a Penny Jar situation.

NOTE Students complete a table and figure out what will happen later in the sequence.

SMH 78, 80

1. Start with: _____

Add each round: _____

2. Complete this table:

Number of Rounds	Total Number of Pennies
Start with	
1	
2	
3	
4	
5	
10	
15	
20	

3. Write an arithmetic expression for how many pennies will be in the jar after 100 rounds.

Backward Problems for Single and Double Towers (page 1 of 2)

Single Towers

Can a single tower ever have exactly this many windows? Circle Yes or No. If yes, write how many floors the tower has.

1. 60 windows?

Yes   No

2. 61 windows?

Yes   No

3. 62 windows?

Yes   No

4. 63 windows?

Yes   No

5. 64 windows?

Yes   No

6. 65 windows?

Yes   No

7. How can you tell whether a single tower can have exactly 105 windows? And if it does, how can you figure out the number of floors it has?

Backward Problems for
Single and Double Towers (page 2 of 2)

Double Towers

Can a double tower ever have exactly this many windows?
Circle Yes or No. If yes, write how many floors the
tower has.

8. 80 windows?

Yes   No

9. 81 windows?

Yes   No

10. 82 windows?

Yes   No

11. 83 windows?

Yes   No

12. 84 windows?

Yes   No

13. 85 windows?

Yes   No

14. How can you tell whether a double tower can have
exactly 108 windows? And if it does, how can you
figure out the number of floors it has?

Square and Corner Towers (page 1 of 2)

Fill in the tables and answer the questions.

Square Towers

Number of Floors	Number of Windows
1	
2	
3	
4	
5	
6	
7	
8	
9	
10	

1. **a.** How did you figure out the number of windows on 10 floors?

   b. Write an arithmetic expression that shows how you figured this out.

2. **a.** How many windows are there on 100 floors?

   b. Write an arithmetic expression that shows how you figured this out.

Square and Corner Towers (page 2 of 2)

Corner Towers

Number of Floors	Number of Windows
1	
2	
3	
4	
5	
6	
7	
8	
9	
10	

3. a. How did you figure out the number of windows on 10 floors?

b. Write an arithmetic expression that shows how you figured this out.

4. a. How many windows are there on 100 floors?

b. Write an arithmetic expression that shows how you figured this out.

Backward Problems for Square and Corner Towers (page 1 of 2)

Square Towers

Can a square tower ever have exactly this many windows?
Circle Yes or No. If yes, write how many floors the
tower has.

1. 90 windows?

Yes   No

2. 91 windows?

Yes   No

3. 92 windows?

Yes   No

4. 93 windows?

Yes   No

5. 94 windows?

Yes   No

6. 95 windows?

Yes   No

7. How can you tell whether a square tower can have
exactly 135 windows? And if it does, how can you
figure out the number of floors it has?

Backward Problems for Square and Corner Towers (page 2 of 2)

Corner Towers

Can a corner tower ever have exactly this many windows?
Circle Yes or No. If yes, write how many floors the
tower has.

8. 90 windows?

Yes   No

9. 91 windows?

Yes   No

10. 92 windows?

Yes   No

11. 93 windows?

Yes   No

12. 94 windows?

Yes   No

13. 95 windows?

Yes   No

14. How can you tell whether a corner tower can have
exactly 123 windows? And if it does, how can you
figure out the number of floors it has?

The Shape of Graphs

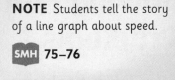

NOTE Students tell the story of a line graph about speed.

SMH 75–76

1. These four graphs each show the speed of a different rider in a long-distance bike ride. Draw a line matching each graph to the description that fits it best.

   a. The rider begins the race by speeding up quickly, then slows down and stays at a mostly steady pace for the rest of the race.

   b. The rider's pace is fastest during the middle of the race.

   c. The rider speeds up and slows down several times during the race.

   d. The rider's pace gets steadily faster as the race goes on.

1

2

3

4

Ongoing Review

2. Which graph shows a rider who ended the race at about the same speed as she began?

   A. Graph 3   **C.** All of the graphs

   B. Graphs 3 and 4   **D.** None of the graphs

Penny Jars and Plant Growth

Homework

Solving Multiplication Problems

NOTE Students practice solving 2-digit multiplication problems.

 40–43

Solve each problem and show your work.

1. $49 \times 25 = $ _____

2. $60 \times 76 = $ _____

3.
$$
\begin{array}{r}
32 \\
\times\ 43 \\
\hline
\end{array}
$$

4.
$$
\begin{array}{r}
78 \\
\times\ 45 \\
\hline
\end{array}
$$

NOTE Students solve
multiplication and division
problems in two ways.

SMH 40–43, 50–52

Solve in Two Ways

Solve each problem in two ways.
Show your solution.

1. $741 \div 19 =$ _____

First way:

Second way:

2. $66 \times 34 =$ _____

First way:

Second way:

Ongoing Review

3. What is the closest estimate of 38×43?

A. 120   **B.** 160   **C.** 1,200   **D.** 1,600

A Table, a Graph, and a Rule (page 1 of 2)

Here is a Penny Jar situation: Start with 26 pennies. Add 4 pennies each round.

NOTE Students are working on making and interpreting tables and graphs. They are also making general rules for finding any number of pennies in the Penny Jar.

SMH 78, 80, 81, 86

1. Make a table to show what happens for 8 rounds. Then graph your data on the following page.

Number of Rounds	Total Number of Pennies
Start with	
1	
2	
3	
4	
5	
6	
7	
8	

2. How many pennies will be in the jar after 30 rounds? Show how you figured this out.

3. Write a rule for the number of pennies for any round. You can use words or an arithmetic expression.

A Table, a Graph, and a Rule (page 2 of 2)

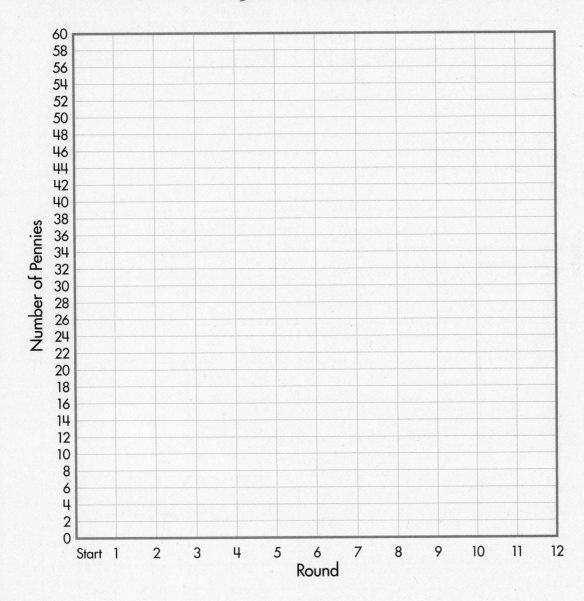

Rules for Towers: Singles and Doubles

1. For a **single** tower, how would you find the number of windows

    a. if there are 20 floors?

    b. if there are 30 floors?

    c. if there are 45 floors?

2. Write a rule for finding the number of windows on a single tower for any number of floors. You can use words or numbers and letters.

3. For a **double** tower, how would you find the number of windows

    a. if there are 20 floors?

    b. if there are 30 floors?

    c. if there are 45 floors?

4. Write a rule for finding the number of windows on a double tower for any number of floors. You can use words or numbers and letters.

Rules for Towers: Corners and Squares

1. For a **corner** tower, how would you find the number of windows

    a. if there are 20 floors?

    b. if there are 30 floors?

    c. if there are 45 floors?

2. Write a rule for finding the number of windows on a corner tower for any number of floors. You can use words or numbers and letters.

3. For a **square** tower, how would you find the number of windows

    a. if there are 20 floors?

    b. if there are 30 floors?

    c. if there are 45 floors?

4. Write a rule for finding the number of windows on a square tower for any number of floors. You can use words or numbers and letters.

Summer Reading

Solve each story problem and show your solutions.

NOTE Students practice solving multiplication and division problems in story problem contexts.

SMH 45

1. Tiana has a new 364-page book to read when she goes on vacation. She is going on vacation for 14 days, and she wants to read the same number of pages each day. How many pages will she read each day?

2. Daniel signed up for a summer reading challenge. He wants to read 75 pages every day in July. There are 31 days in July. How many pages will he read in July?

3. Kate plans to read 35 pages every day in July and 40 pages every day in August. There are 31 days in August, too.

a. How many pages will Kate read in July?

b. How many pages will Kate read in August?

Penny Jar Problems (page 1 of 2)

NOTE Students are using tables to help them think about number relationships.

SMH **80**

1. Fill out the table for the following Penny Jar situation: Start with 2 pennies. Add 4 pennies each round.

Number of Rounds	Number of Pennies
Start with	
1	
2	
3	
4	
5	

2. Is there ever a round when you will have exactly 50 pennies in the Penny Jar? If so, what round will that be? How do you know?

3. Is there ever a round when you will have exactly 51 pennies in the Penny Jar? If so, what round will that be? How do you know?

Penny Jar Problems (page 2 of 2)

4. Which of these amounts cannot be in the jar:
52, 53, or 54 pennies?

5. Choose one number that will be in the Penny Jar
and explain how you know.

6. Choose one number that you know can never be
in the Penny Jar and explain how you know.

Fast and Slow Growth

1. **a.** Where does this graph show the **fastest** growth? Circle this on the graph.

   b. How can you tell from the **shape** of the graph?

   c. How can you tell from the **numbers** along the graph?

Day	Height
Thursday	3 cm
Friday	4 cm
Monday	10 cm
Tuesday	13.5 cm
Wednesday	15 cm
Thursday	16 cm
Friday	16.5 cm
Monday	17 cm

2. **a.** Where does this graph show the **slowest** growth? Circle this on the graph.

   b. How can you tell from the **shape** of the graph?

   c. How can you tell from the **numbers** along the graph?

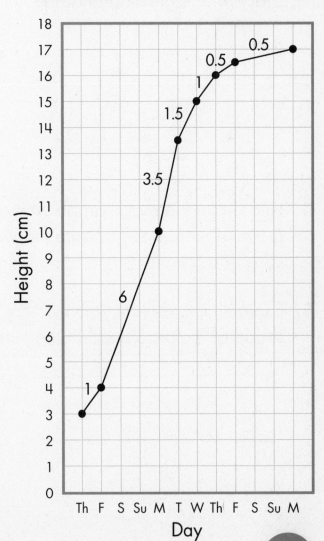

Our Growing Plants

Use this sheet with the graph you have made
of your growing plant.

1. On the graph of your growing plant, write the changes
(in centimeters) on each section of the line.

2. Find a place on your graph where your plant was
growing quickly. Write the word "fast" along your
graph in this place.

3. Explain how you know this is fast growth. Look at the
shape of the graph and at the numbers on your graph.

4. Find a place on your graph where your plant was
growing more slowly. Write the word "slow" along
your graph in this place.

5. Explain how you know this is slow growth. Look at the
shape of the graph and at the numbers on your graph.

Daily Practice

Whose Graph Is It?

In the famous race between a tortoise and a hare, the hare sped off and was so confident that he could win the race that he took time for a nap!

Meanwhile, the tortoise kept a slow but steady pace. By the time the hare woke up and started running again, the tortoise was just crossing the finish line.

> **NOTE** Students tell the story of a line graph about speed.
>
> SMH 75–76

1. Which graph shows the tortoise's speed?
Which shows the hare's speed?
Explain your thinking.

A.   **B.**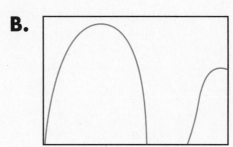

_____

_____

_____

_____

2. Circle True or False about the following statement:
Even though the tortoise won the race, his ending speed was slower than the hare's ending speed.

   A. True   **B.** False

Writing Multiplication Story Problems

NOTE Students practice solving 2-digit multiplication problems.

SMH 40–43

For each problem, write a story problem. Then solve the problem and show your solution.

1. $82 \times 39 = $ _____

Story problem:

Solution:

2. $56 \times 91 = $ _____

Story problem:

Solution:

A Plant Story

The plant graph shown here has been divided into six parts.

NOTE Students tell the story of a line graph about plant growth.

 SMH 75–77

1. Write a story that makes sense for each part of the plant's growth. Part A has been done for you.

Part A: The plant started growing slowly.

Part B: _____

Part C: _____

Part D: _____

Part E: _____

Part F: _____

A B C D E F

Ongoing Review

2. Which sequence describes the changes shown in the graph?

   A. + + + 0 − − +

   B. − + + + − − +

   C. − + + 0 − − +

   D. 0 + + 0 − − 0

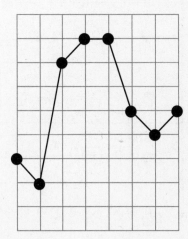

Division Practice

Solve each division problem.
Then write the related
multiplication combination.

NOTE Students are reviewing division problems that are related to the multiplication combinations they know.

SMH 35

Division Problem	Multiplication Combination
1. $144 \div 12 =$ _____	_____ × _____ = _____
2. $32 \div 8 =$ _____	_____ × _____ = _____
3. $28 \div 4 =$ _____	_____ × _____ = _____
4. $56 \div 7 =$ _____	_____ × _____ = _____
5. $110 \div 11 =$ _____	_____ × _____ = _____
6. $64 \div 8 =$ _____	_____ × _____ = _____
7. $63 \div 9 =$ _____	_____ × _____ = _____
8. $27 \div 3 =$ _____	_____ × _____ = _____
9. $7\overline{)49}$	_____ × _____ = _____
10. $9\overline{)81}$	_____ × _____ = _____

Pizza Problems

Solve each story problem and show your solutions. You may also use a picture to explain your thinking.

NOTE Students practice solving multistep story problems involving multiplication and division.

1. There are 11 people at a pizza party. Each person wants 3 slices of pizza, and each pizza has 8 slices. How many pizzas should they order?

2. At a larger pizza party, there are 18 people. Each person wants 3 slices, and each pizza has 8 slices. How many pizzas should they order?

3. At a smaller pizza party, there are 7 people. They order 3 pizzas. Each person eats 3 slices, and each pizza has 8 slices. How much extra pizza do they have?

A Penny Jar Story (page 1 of 2)

Here is a Penny Jar situation: Start with
1 penny. Add 3 pennies each round.

> **NOTE** Students make a table
> and a graph for a Penny Jar
> situation. They also show how
> they would figure out what
> happens after round 20.
>
> **SMH** 80–81

1. Make a table for the first 8 rounds
of this Penny Jar situation:

2. How many pennies will be in the jar after 20 rounds?
Show how you figured this out.

A Penny Jar Story (page 2 of 2)

3. Make a graph of the Penny Jar situation in Problem 2.

Removing Pennies
from a Penny Jar (page 1 of 2)

Here is a Penny Jar situation: Start with 95 pennies.
Remove 4 pennies each round.

1. Make a table to show what happens for 8 rounds.

Number of Rounds	Number of Pennies
Start with	
1	
2	
3	
4	
5	
6	
7	
8	

2. Make a graph of this Penny Jar situation on the
next page.

3. When will there be 0 pennies in the jar?
Show how you figured this out.

Removing Pennies from a Penny Jar (page 2 of 2)

Number of Pennies

Round

Comparing Graphs

The pairs of graphs show plant growth.
Circle the answer to each question.

NOTE Students interpret the shape of line graphs about plant growth.

 75–77

1. Which plant grew more quickly?		
2. Which plant is taller?		
3. Which plant had its top broken off?		
4. Which plant stopped growing?		

Ongoing Review

5. Which of the following is the most likely story of this graph?

A. A Plant's Growth

B. A Runner's Speed

C. A Penny Jar Situation

D. The Temperature on a Hot Day

More Division Practice

Solve each division problem.
Then write the related multiplication
combination.

NOTE Students are reviewing division
problems that are related to the
multiplication combinations they know.

SMH 35

Division Problem	Multiplication Combination
1. $7\overline{)42}$	_____ × _____ = _____
2. $72 \div 6 =$ _____	_____ × _____ = _____
3. $8\overline{)48}$	_____ × _____ = _____
4. $108 \div 9 =$ _____	_____ × _____ = _____
5. $60 \div 12 =$ _____	_____ × _____ = _____
6. $36 \div 6 =$ _____	_____ × _____ = _____
7. $12\overline{)96}$	_____ × _____ = _____
8. $63 \div 7 =$ _____	_____ × _____ = _____
9. $72 \div 9 =$ _____	_____ × _____ = _____
10. $9\overline{)54}$	_____ × _____ = _____

Representing Constant Change

NOTE Students solve real-world problems involving the math content of this unit.

SMH 86

Steve earns $0.50 day for feeding his family's dog and making his bed. He wants to save $10.00 to buy some trading cards. He starts with $3.00.

Number of Days	Amount Saved
Start	$3.00
1	
2	
3	
4	
5	
10	
15	

How many days will it take him to earn enough money if he does his chores every day?

Write an arithmetic expression to show how much money he will have saved after 30 days.